# WAR AND PEACE

*The Survival of the Talbots of Malahide 1641–1671*

# Maynooth Studies in Local History

GENERAL EDITOR Raymond Gillespie

This is one of the new pamphlets published in 1997 in the Maynooth Studies in Local History series. Like earlier titles in the series, published in 1995 and 1996, each study is derived from a thesis completed in connection with the Maynooth M.A. course in local history.

The localities studied are defined not by administrative boundaries but by the nature of the community bonds which shaped people's experiences in the past, both holding them together and driving them apart. Ranging across family, village, parish, town, and estate, the pamphlets investigate how people in these varied communities lived out their lives and responded to changes in the outside world.

These Maynooth Studies in Local History explore the richness and diversity of the Irish historical experience, and in doing so present local history as the vibrant and challenging discipline that it is.

*Maynooth Studies in Local History: Number 13*

# War and Peace

## *The Survival of the Talbots of Malahide 1641–1671*

## Joseph Byrne

IRISH ACADEMIC PRESS

Set in 10 on 12 point Bembo by
Carrigboy Typesetting Services, Co. Cork
and published by
IRISH ACADEMIC PRESS LTD
Northumberland House
44, Northumberland Road, Ballsbridge, Dublin 4, Ireland
*and in North America by*
IRISH ACADEMIC PRESS LTD
c/o ISBS, 5804 NE Hassalo Street, Portland, OR 97123

A catalogue record for this title
is available from the British Library.

ISBN 0-7165-2629-8

Printed in Ireland
by ColourBooks, Dublin

# Contents

FIGURES

LIST OF TABLES

NOTES

All acreage figures are expressed in Irish (or Plantation) measure, 1 Irish acre equalling 1.62 statute acres. Dates are given according to New Style for the year but Old Style for the day and month. Money amounts have been decimalised in the appendices.

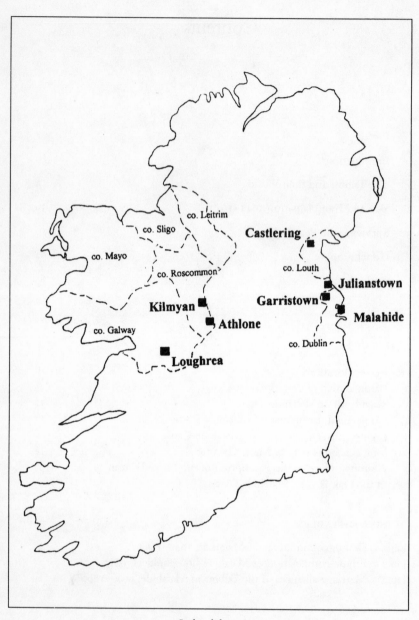

*1*. Ireland, locations

# Preface

I would like to express my gratitude to the library staffs of the National Library of Ireland, the Bodleian Library, Oxford, Dublin Corporation Gilbert Library, Trinity College, Dublin, St Patrick's College, Maynooth, St. Patrick's College, Drumcondra and to the staff of the National Archives. I am particularly indebted to Harold O'Sullivan for sharing his in-depth knowledge of the Cromwellian and Restoration land settlements. I would like to thank Tom O'Shea for placing his collection of Talbotiana at my disposal and for permission to use some of that material to illustrate this study. William Salters Sterling, executor to the late Jocelyn Otway-Ruthven, was inordinately accommodating and gracious in granting me access to the Calendar of Talbot Mss, which Professor Otway-Ruthven had brought to an advanced stage of editing prior to her decease. I would like to acknowledge the contribution of Dr. Raymond Gillespie, whose encouragement, criticism and direction proved invaluable in the preparation of this study. Finally, I would like to thank Siobhan, Stephen and Lisa for their patience and understanding.

2. Baronial map of county Dublin, 1655.

# Introduction

By the mid-seventeenth century the lordship of Malahide, county Dublin, had been in the possession of the Talbots, an Old English Catholic family, for almost five hundred years. The Talbot estate had been augmented in the late fifteenth century by a royal grant of the customs of the port of Malahide and by the purchase of the manors of Garristown, county Dublin, and Castlering, county Louth. Rooted firmly in the society of the Pale, the Talbots were linked to their fellow Old English Catholics through a highly developed network of social, political, economic and religious ties. The outbreak of war in Ulster in 1641 rapidly engaged the Old English Catholics of the Pale and the conflict which followed presented the Talbots with a crisis unparalleled in their history. Though staunch royalists, they were outlawed in the 1640s, imprisoned and transplanted by the Commonwealth during the 1650s and family estates were sequestrated and granted to Cromwellian soldiers and adventurers. In this they were not unique. In the course of the seventeenth century, historians have estimated that Catholic landownership declined from sixty one per cent in 1641 to twenty two per cent in 1688 and by the turn of the century was as low as fifteen per cent.[1] Traditionally, as Raymond Gillespie observes, this decline has been attributed to the impact of plantation, the Restoration land settlement and the Williamite confiscations.[2] The difficulty with this view is that it conveys an image of Catholic landowners as passive victims of anti-Catholic forces and ignores the fact that many Catholics carried with them into the turmoil of the mid-seventeenth century a broad range of social, economic, cultural and political baggage which enabled them to adapt to, accommodate and survive the drastic religious and political change of the period. Thus, while many of their Old English Catholic neighbours, the Blackneys, the Gouldings, the Kings, the Nettervilles of Kilcrea, the Caddells, the Cruises and the Travers, suffered a terminal loss of their estates and disappeared from the proprietorial class of the region, the Talbots and many others survived. The Talbot crisis was most acute under John Talbot, lord of Malahide from 1640. When he died in 1671 the bulk of the estate was still in the hands of former Cromwellians but Malahide and a portion of the Garristown land had been successfully recovered. This study is an attempt to explain how John Talbot managed to overcome the devastating setbacks inflicted on Talbot fortunes between 1641 and his death in 1671.

The key source to the history of the Talbots of Malahide in the seventeenth century is the collection of estate papers in the Bodleian Library. While the

Talbot papers contain but a slender run of seventeenth century documents, the general contours of the mid-century crisis can be traced through a cluster of material comprising inquisitions *post-mortem*, wills, petitions, suits in the court of exchequer, certificates and decrees of innocence and other miscellaneous material. Sadly, the focus within these documents is always on a picture wider than the internal operations of the Talbot manor of Malahide. The lack of leases for the sixteenth and seventeenth centuries, for example, means that the functioning of the manor of Malahide can only be accessed by analogy with Garristown, for which a sprinkling of early seventeenth century leases survive, or through a retrospective reading of late seventeenth and early eighteenth century documents and leases. The absence of contemporary personal documents, a notable exception being a rhapsody on the carving of the assumption of the Blessed Virgin in the Oak Room at Malahide, is a serious but not fatal blow.[3] A range of other sources, including the early volumes of the Carte and the Ormonde manuscripts and the State Papers-Ireland, compensate for this deficit by documenting the activities of John Talbot during the war, and, in doing so, provide a valuable entree into the Talbot mentality. The visit of John Dunton, a London bookseller, to Malahide in 1698, recalled in *Teague land, or a merry ramble to the wild Irish: letters from Ireland, 1698*, offers a rare insight into the social and cultural life of the town of Malahide in the seventeenth century.

At a broader level the impact of the land settlements of the 1650s and 1660s on the Talbots can be accessed through a range of official sources. The implementation of the changes in landownership foreshadowed by the Adventurers' Act (1642) and enacted in the Cromwellian (1652) and Restoration (1662) Acts of Settlement necessitated the taking of a whole series of nationwide surveys, the Gross, Civil and Down Surveys, an ongoing administrative framework to chart those changes, preserved in the books of survey and distribution, together with legal mechanisms, the courts of claims of 1663 and 1666-9, to process the claims of innocents. These sources are accessible through *The Civil Survey, A.D. 1654–56*, (1931–61), in ten volumes, *The Transplantation to Connacht, 1654–58*, (1970), and *Books of survey and distribution*, (1944–67), four volumes dealing with counties in Connacht, all of which were edited by Robert Simington. For counties Dublin and Louth, where the Talbot estates were situated, the Quit Rent Office set of the books of survey and distribution preserved in the National Archives and the parish maps of the Down Survey (Ms 714) in the National Library complement that material. J.G. Simms's transcript of the Armagh Public Library manuscript, 'Claims of innocence: submissions and evidence, 28 January–20 August 1663', on deposit in Trinity College, Dublin, contains Talbot submissions to the first court of claims and reveals the legal strategies the Talbots employed to retrieve their inheritance. The destruction of the official records of the Commonwealth regime in the fire in the Four Courts in 1922 created an evidential gap which is only partially filled by a number of collections of transcripts, Robert Dunlop's two-volume selection being a valuable example.[4] Inevitably these selections focus on a level wider than the local community and so the only way in which the impact of the Cromwellian period on the Talbots and Malahide can be accessed is by trawling through a disparate range of sources in the hope that cumulatively they can be condensed into a meaningful history.

While there have been national studies of the effects of the Cromwellian and Restoration settlements on landownership, very little work has been done at county level. In this regard, L.J. Arnold's study of the Restoration land settlement in county Dublin and, especially, Harold O'Sullivan's doctoral thesis on landownership changes in seventeenth century county Louth contribute significantly to our understanding of the complex mechanisms by which the land settlements were implemented.[5] If studies at county level have been somewhat neglected, even less attention again has been focused on the effects of these settlements on smaller communities. Yet it is only at that level that the patchwork implementation of the settlements can be understood. How did families like the Talbots of Malahide survive while others, like the Blackneys of nearby Rickenhore, disappeared? Raymond Gillespie's essay on the O'Farrells of Longford, cited above, goes a considerable way towards providing a blueprint for micro-studies of the period at local level in demonstrating how an understanding of the reasons for survival depends to a large degree on a consideration of the cultural background from which those survival strategies evolved.

The first part of this study explores the physical, economic, social, political and religious fabric of the Talbots' world. A reconstruction of the Talbot world should contribute towards an understanding of the extent to which John Talbot was equipped to meet the challenges presented by the 1641 rebellion and the turmoil which followed. Part two considers Talbot's demeanour during the war, the accommodations he made in order to maintain the integrity of his inheritance and his reaction to transplantation under the Commonwealth regime. Finally, the third section investigates the complex post-Restoration process of manoeuvring through which Talbot attempted to retrieve his estate from the powerful competing Protestant interests to whom Talbot property had been granted during the 1650s and 1660s.

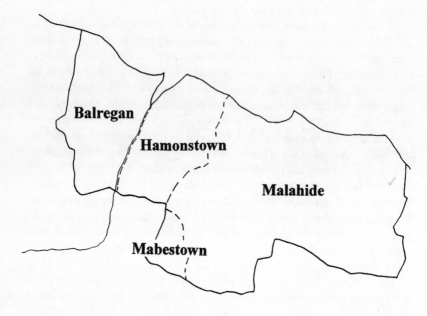

3. Townlands of Malahide, 1641

# The Talbots of Malahide and their World

In July 1640, upon the death of his father Richard, John Talbot succeeded to the lordship of the Talbot estates. His inheritance comprised the county Dublin manors of Malahide (605 acres) and Garristown (1,390 acres), together with the county Louth manor of Castlering (1,845 acres), in extent a total of 3,840 acres.[1] Approximately half of the Garristown lands were assigned to Elizabeth Talbot, Richard's widow, as her dowry, and remained as such until the late 1650s when they were granted to Alexander Staples, a Cromwellian officer.[2] Malahide is situated in Fingal, north county Dublin, a region comprising the ancient baronies of Coolock, Nethercross and Balrothery. The English antiquarian William Camden, writing in 1607, described Fingal as 'a little country, but very good and passing well husbanded; even the garner and barn of this kingdom, so great store of corn it yeeldeth every year'.[3]

The manor of Malahide, situated on the southern shore of the Broadmeadow estuary, contained four townlands (figure 3). These were Malahide itself, which included the demesne lands, the town and port of that name and the coastal strip eastwards, the townlands of Balregan and Hamonstown or Hamonswood (both forming the modern townland of Yellow Walls) in the west and the tiny townland of Mabestown to the south. Physically the manor land is dominated by Malahide Hill (57m) which bisects the eastern portion of the land, running parallel to the coastline as far as the town, while the land to the west slopes gently northwards to the sea. Malahide is traversed by a single stream, the diminutive Gaybrook, which flows northwards through a cutting into the estuary at Yellow Walls, but its hillside setting ensures that the land is efficiently drained. John Rocque's map of Malahide shows the manor to have a well-established *bocage* landscape by 1760 but as the Talbot estate papers contain no sixteenth or seventeenth century leases on Malahide it is difficult to determine the extent to which enclosure was a feature of the local landscape in the 1600s. Thomas Balle's 1495 lease of 'four acres more or less of tilling land *to make a park*' suggests that the process of enclosure was certainly underway by the late fifteenth century.[4]

Estimated by the Civil Survey commissioners to contain 500 acres (in fact it contained over 605 acres), the manor of Malahide appears at first glance to have been a tiny estate.[5] By the standards of county Dublin, however, this was not the case for estates there tended to be relatively small. Excluding common land, bog and the coastal strip of connywarrens, the Civil Survey commissioners estimated the combined baronies of Coolock, Nethercross and Balrothery to contain 48,489 acres which, when averaged out amongst the 148 proprietors who held estates there, yields an average estate size of 327 acres. Thus, the manor of Malahide exceeded the average estate size for the Fingal region and in extent ranked twenty-ninth (Appendix 1). Ranking by acreage is a rather poor determinant of the value of an estate, however, for in a region already favourably advantaged by the fertility of the soil, there were significant inter-baronial differences. The quality of land deteriorates as it rises northwards from the city towards Balrothery, a fact which is reflected in the differing valuations assigned by the commissioners to similarly sized estates. Matthew Barnewall's 587 acre estate in the barony of Balrothery, for example, was calculated to be worth an estimated £152.15 in rental value yearly whereas John Talbot's 500 acre Malahide estate in the barony of Coolock was rated at £300 yearly.[6] It appears that one required to own at least twice as much land in Balrothery in order to generate a similar annual rental to Talbot's Malahide estate. Hence, when the 148 estates are ranked according to estimated yearly value, Talbot's estate rises to thirteenth place in the pecking order (Appendix 2). As a criterion to determine profitability, however, estimated yearly rental value obscures the underlying profitability of individual estates. Nicholas Barnewall, the leading landowner in Fingal, held 4,017.5 acres with an estimated annual rental value of £1308.5 but the bulk of Barnewall's estate lay in the poorer barony of Balrothery so that his average rating per acre was £0.32. Talbot's Malahide, in extent but one-eighth of Barnewall's, and rated at less than one-quarter of his estimated annual rental value, was calculated to generate a return of £0.59 per acre. Effectively, his land was almost twice as profitable per acre as Barnewall's. Applying the criterion of profitability per acre to the schedule of Fingallian proprietors, the manor of Malahide rises dramatically to third position in the scale (Appendix 3). Apart from its location in the more fertile Coolock barony and its proximity to the city of Dublin, Talbot's high profitability ratio per acre was attributable to the fact that, unlike many other large estates which tended to comprise multiple dispersed holdings, the Malahide estate was consolidated into a single holding. The estates of seventy four proprietors, or fifty per cent of the total, contained two or more holdings. Barnewall's 4,017 acres, for example, were dispersed in thirty separate holdings, spread across the three Fingallian baronies. Despite its diminutive size, then, Malahide was nevertheless a substantially lucrative estate.

In the seventeenth century there were two main areas of settlement within the manor. These were the environs of the manor house, Malahide Court, and about one mile to the north, the main settlement, the town of Malahide. The accretions and alterations of several centuries have dramatically transformed the original manor house but the surviving physical evidence, the records of the Civil and Down Surveys and the Talbot estate papers enable a relatively good reconstruction of the house as it appeared in 1640 to be effected (figure 4).

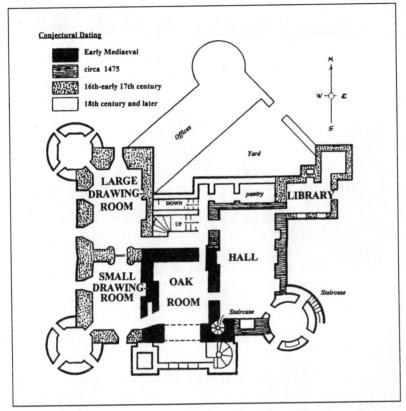

4. Conjectural dating plan of Malahide Castle.

The core of the building, a three storey keep of which but three walls and a circular staircase remain, derives probably from the fifteenth century. The great hall and the adjoining late medieval parish church were added late in the century, probably about 1475, a period contemporaneous with the royal grant of the manor, the customs and admiralty of the port and the acquisition by purchase of the manors of Garristown and Castlering. The west wing was added about 1600.[7] There is no evidence to suggest that any further additions were made by the 1650s when the Civil Survey commissioners described the manor house as 'a faire Stone house slated with several other Office houses slated, some Ash trees about the house for ornament'.[8] A hollow below the western wall of the modern castle suggests that the original 'keep' was moated, the moated sections on the other sides being later infilled to accommodate eighteenth century enlargements.

A ditch, occasionally a double ditch, which presently encircles the castle, constituted part of the defensive outworks. A sketch map of the castle drawn

MALLAHIDE-CASTLE in the Co: of DUBLIN.

5. Eighteenth-century view of Malahide Castle.

in 1846 by James Talbot as he recollected it to be in 1775, indicates that the bank
of the ditch was walled. Writing to his son James, he observed that there was
also a moat, 'probably without the wall'.[9] In 1861 his sister Charlotte recalled
that when her mother first came to Malahide (c.1765), 'there were outward
walls and towers but in a ruinous state'.[10] A single tower standing in the walled
garden to the east of the castle is a remnant of this fortification. Unlike the modern entrance which is on the south side of the building, the main entrance to
the castle was originally on the eastern side, facing the village (figure 5). Entry
was gained by means of a drawbridge and beneath a portcullis into the courtyard which was guarded by a barbican.[11]

Within the walled area or bawn, James Talbot's sketch includes an outline
of the manor prison together with some offices, stables, a barn and the medieval church and graveyard. Rocque's map (1760) authenticates the testimony
of these memoirs showing the prison and stables and an extensive walled area
(figure 6). The original keep appears to have constituted the final defence in
a network whose chief aim was to forestall pillaging by the native Irish tribes.
In this they were not entirely successful for in 1554 a raiding party of the
O'Byrnes and the O'Tooles, having failed to take Howth, surprised the
Talbots 'and burst open the gates till they came to the hall door where ... they
were resisted with great difficulty'.[12] Nevertheless, during the Confederate

insurrection of the 1640s Malahide Court was considered sufficiently stout to be employed as a royalist garrison. In March 1642, the duke of Ormonde, commander-in-chief of the royalist forces, occupied the castle and wrote to the lords justice in Dublin, 'on my coming to this place and viewing it[s] site and strength thereof I consulted with Sr. Symon Harcourt, Sr. Thomas Lucas and other ye officers who are of opinion that a garrison of 200 men is fitt to be left here, it will be good accommodation for them and they of strength enough to keep ye place'. [13] Thus Malahide Court, a fortification designed to lock out the native Irish, became part of the mid-seventeenth century chain of garrisons across the north inner Pale whose express purpose was to deny access to the city not only to the native Irish but also to the Old English rebels.

In extent, the seventeenth century Court was probably one of the largest of its kind in Fingal. Containing eleven hearths in 1663, it was surpassed by only five houses in the region. [14] Internally, the concept of personal privacy, manifested later by the partitioning of open areas and the insertion of doors, appears to have been only partially established. James Talbot observed that the rooms on the first floor were originally divided into four, to which there were no doors, the entrances being closed by tapestry hangings. [15] Entrance to the house was gained from the courtyard into the great hall by way of a flight of steps. The great hall was probably the centre of daily activity in the manor house, superseding the original living quarters in the Oak Room which was situated on the first floor of the 'keep'. This latter room, panelled throughout in oak, contains a sixteenth-century Flemish carving of the assumption of the Blessed Virgin into heaven affixed to the chimney-breast, the dominant position of the icon reflecting the high status accorded her by the Talbots and the distinctive Marian orientation of their religious devotion. Post-Restoration alterations to the structure and appearance of the old building, which included the raising of floors and ceilings and the lengthening of windows, diminished its stature as a fortification. [16] Taken together with the removal of the outer defenceworks, these alterations suggest an attempt to gentrify the Court and, with the memory of the Ormonde occupation yet vivid, a deliberate attempt to diminish the attractiveness of Malahide Court to potential military occupiers.

As regards the configuration of the town, a strong case can also be made for reading Rocque's 1760 map into the evidential record (figure 6). Rocque, as we have seen, authenticated written evidence in relation to the castle fortifications. More significantly, a substantial body of eighteenth century Talbot leases exists for the lands of Malahide but those which deal with the town and the development of the modern streetscape appear exclusively in the last decades of that century, at least twenty years after Rocque had mapped the area. Thus, Rocque's map appears to reflect the streetscape of the seventeenth century town. Three streets radiated from the central 'square' in what is now Old Street, one heading west before turning sharply south towards the castle

6. John Rocque's map of Malahide, 1760.

and thence onwards to the city, a second heading south-eastwards, passing through the Grange of Portmarnock also in the direction of the city and the third inclined to the estuary where, directly opposite an extensive oyster fishery, it forked eastwards and westwards along the shoreline. Strung out along the shore were the fishermen's houses, those furthest along the western coastline possessing large 'backsides', while those nearest the centre, by reason of backing on to others, having much smaller rear gardens.

In the centre of the square Rocque maps the source of the town's water supply, the well known variously as the Sunday Well, the Lady Well or St. Sylvester's Well, the location for the annual Marian pattern.[17] While the physical evidence has long disappeared, the port appears to have contained a formal quayside for in a detailed submission to the court of claims in 1663, Jane Talbot, John's sister, claimed an interest in the 'shipworks' at Malahide.[18] One of the earliest accounts of the appearance of the town is given by John Dunton, a London bookseller, who frequented Malahide in the late 1690s. To eyes more accustomed to the English style, the first sight of Malahide was an affront:

> About two miles farther the town of Malahide saluted our eyes with the best figure it could make, because the nearer we approached it the worse it appeared … It contains about thirty ordinary huts in all, and not one without several little children who were sprawling about the fireplace (for there was but small appearance of fire on it) like so many maggots on a dunghill in a summer's day.[19]

Unlike the Court and its offices which were stone-built and slated, the Civil Survey notes that almost all the houses in the town were thatched and by implication, mud-walled, for the only stone-built thatched building recorded there was the house of Thomas Jones.[20]

Attempts to quantify the mid-seventeenth century population of Malahide are fraught with difficulty for the key demographic sources for the period, the poll tax lists and the hearth money rolls, were largely destroyed in 1922. For county Dublin, only the 1660 poll tax parish aggregates and the 1663 hearth money rolls survive.[21] As conclusions drawn from counties in Ulster (for which a more complete schedule of hearth and poll tax returns survives) reveal, a high incidence of evasion and exemption ensures that these sources are most reliable only in establishing minimum population levels.[22] To complicate matters, the population of Malahide was skewed during the early 1640s by the garrisoning of two hundred soldiers and again from 1653 when Malahide Court was occupied by Miles Corbet, chief baron of the exchequer.[23] Other sources, such as inquisitions *post-mortem* and the Civil Survey (1654–6), also provide some demographic evidence but their accuracy is no less questionable. Richard Talbot's inquisition *post-mortem* taken in November 1640, for example, shows that he died seised of a mansion house and twenty messuages in Malahide.[24] The Civil Survey return for Malahide suggests a slight increase,

noting 'in ye Towne of Mullahide about twenty Thatcht houses One Sea
Water Mill, Also one Stone thatcht house with two small thatcht houses in
possession of Thomas Jones'.[25] By 1663, however, the hearth rolls show thirty-
five houses liable for the hearth levy which, at first glance, suggests an increase
of seventy-five per cent in housing stock, a phenomenal growth rate for a
seven-year (albeit plague and famine free) period.[26] In fact all three returns
probably understate the size of the village. An inquisition *post-mortem* was typically conducted, as Talbot's was, by estimation. The Civil Survey, effectively a
manorial inquisition writ large to embrace the entire country, was conducted
on a similar basis. Secondly, both estimations appear to refer to different settlement types, the inquisition *post-mortem* to messuages, houses with gardens,
within the entire manor, whereas the Civil Survey appears to concentrate only
on the cabins within the town. Both figures therefore probably constitute the
minimum number of houses within the bounds of the manor. As the Hearth
Tax Act of 1662 exempted persons living on alms or not able to live by work
or those whose houses or property failed to reach a certain minimum value,
the 1663 hearth rolls also probably understate the number of households in
the manor.[27] That there were exemptions in Malahide appears beyond doubt.
The poll tax returns for 1660 which record all adults above the age of fifteen
years show that 118 inhabitants of Malahide were liable for this tax.[28] Arguing
that the population of Ireland in 1672 was roughly three times the number of
persons contained in the poll tax returns, L.M. Cullen suggests that a multiplier of three applied to poll tax lists should generate a rough indication of
population.[29] In the case of Malahide this would imply a population of 354 or
an average household size of 10.1 residents. Given the widely accepted average household size of 4.5 to 5.5 for the period, this figure appears somewhat
high.[30] However, when one multiplies the number of houses liable for the
hearth tax by the more generous of the latter figures, the resulting population
at 192 seems excessively small when compared with the poll list total of 118
adults. This suggests that either a substantial number of houses were exempted
from or evaded the hearth tax or that the manor experienced a dramatic
slump in population after 1660. A decline in population would reconcile the
apparent contradiction between the poll tax and hearth roll returns and there
is evidence to suggest that this, in fact, is what occurred.

   In 1653, Miles Corbet, fleeing from the plague in Dublin, ousted John Talbot
from Malahide Court and settled with his family there.[31] Corbet's removal to
Malahide appears to have triggered the growth of a small colony of officials,
retainers and soldiers in the neighbourhood of the castle. Richard Cotton, for
example, described as a 'titulado' in the Malahide poll list alongside Corbet and
his son, was a commissioner for the implementation of the poll tax.[32]
Additionally, from October 1653, the Commonwealth farmed the customs of
Malahide (and all the other ports of county Dublin) to Ralph Hughes who
appointed his own officials there.[33] Thus the 1660 poll tax list records thirty-

six English (using Cullen's multiplier, the equivalent of 108 English residents of all ages) among the 118 adults in Malahide who were liable for the tax. The poll tax list probably reflects the moment at which the population of Malahide peaked for in December 1659, as the Commonwealth government crumbled, Corbet fled to England. With the Restoration imminent and their association with the regicide Commonwealth commissioner now perhaps lacking the cachet it once held, many of the English may also have de-camped. Cotton appears to have left Malahide after the collection of the poll tax (April–July 1660) as his name disappears from the schedule of commissioners for 1661, and Ralph Hughes's appointment was annulled and the post given to Thomas Worsopp.[34] In the light of an exodus of Corbet's retinue from about 1660 the hearth tax roll listing of thirty-five houses at Malahide and a possible population of about 192 by 1663 begins to make sense. Dunton's 1698 observation that the town of Malahide contained about 'thirty ordinary huts' suggests that the demography of Malahide altered little from the 1660s to the close of the seventeenth century.[35] When presented in tabular form (Table 1) and the temporary population surges which attended the occupations are ignored, it appears that there was a substantial underlying increase in the population and housing stock between 1640 and 1660.

*Table 1: Tentative Demographic Summary of Malahide, 1640–1698*[36]

|  | Houses | Population | |
|---|---|---|---|
| 1640 | 20+ | 110+ | |
| 1642–3 | 20+ | 310+ | (includes military garrison of 200) |
| 1654–60 | 23+ | 354+ | (Corbet occupation) |
| 1663 | 35+ | 192+ | |
| 1698 | 30+ | 192+ | |

Ethnically, as Table 2 illustrates, the householders listed in the 1663 hearth money rolls appear to spring equally from Old English and native Irish origins.

*Table 2: Ethnic composition of Malahide householders, 1663*[37]

| Old English (17) | | Irish (18) | | |
|---|---|---|---|---|
| Talbot | Jones | Daley | Gowran | Graffan |
| Fagan | Edwards(4) | Brady | Brennan | Sherkey |
| Bruton | Gaggers | Rely (2) | Durnine | Roaney |
| Archbold | Howard (2) | Kelly | Doyle | |
| Carr | Rickard | Laughlin | Keane | |
| Dollard | Ellis | Maneihan | Tagon | |
| Dalton | | Connor | Hamill | |

Dunton's account of his visit to Malahide, taken together with the evidence of the ethnic composition of the town, suggests that the townspeople were probably bilingual. While the bulk of his communications with local people were conducted in English, Dunton also recorded evidence of the use of Gaelic in the town. Arriving in Malahide on Easter Monday, 1698, he came upon the local priest who appears to have introduced himself both in Gaelic and English:'One Father Gowan, or Smith as he called himself, a la mode de Angleterre, happened to be at the inn when we arrived ...'.[38] Later in the day Dunton was entertained in Gaelic by the innkeeper's wife:'Even our landlady was brought in to sing an Irish Cronaan, which is so odd a thing that I cannot express it, being mostly performed in the throat only now and then some miserable sounds are sent through the nose'.[39] The ability to speak English would have been a valuable asset, given the trading links with the fish markets in Dublin and with the ports of west Britain, for the inhabitants of the town were heavily engaged in that trade. Ormonde certainly regarded Malahide as a 'fisher town' and the surveyors of the Down Survey concurred, noting that 'Mallahide contains ... many thatched houses and cabbins by the seaside or bay, where fishermen dwelleth'.[40]

Although fish was clearly a staple of consumption, the evidence of Dunton's brief sojourn at the inn of Malahide suggests that the local diet was by no means limited. Dunton was served 'salt fish and eggs, hen and bacon, and rabbits'.[41] The inventory of the Malahide fisherman, John Mold, suggests that sheep were also raised near Malahide.[42] Thus within the neighbourhood of the town, poultry, pigs and sheep were kept and rabbit could be procured from the warren by the seashore. The diet at the manor house was probably even more varied yet the kitchen habits at the Court failed to impress Bridget, the English wife of Sir John Talbot and kinswoman of the earl of Shrewsbury. In 1594 she wrote to the countess of Shrewsbury asking that one of her servants be allowed to work for a time in the Shrewsbury kitchen under the master cook.[43] In *The Dublin Scuffle* (1699), Dunton describes Malahide as 'a place as eminent as Billingsgate for people going to eat oysters there'.[44] Malahide, however, appears to have been poorly equipped to meet the liquid needs of day-trippers from the capital. It possessed but one inn, 'a poor ordinary place' and the quality of alcoholic beverages on offer was clearly suspect.[45] A saying he had overheard in Dublin, 'If you go to Malahide bring a bottle by your side', was interpreted by Dunton to imply that it was difficult to get a drink there.[46] In fact, as his own experience proved, the saying more properly reflected the general disrepute in which the local liquor was held. He noted that when ale was served at the inn the maid 'poured some into a glass and drank it off'.[47] This custom, he was informed, was designed 'to take away any suspicion of poison being in the liquor'.

Malahide was granted manorial status in 1475 and the manor court continued to function until such courts were abolished in the mid-nineteenth century.[48] A manor court of such longevity should have produced a considerable amount of evidence in the form of rentals, leases, court rolls and surveys, but very little has survived to facilitate a reconstruction of its daily functioning. The manorial grant to Thomas Talbot in 1475 entitled him to hold a court leet and court baron. [49] This entitled the lord of Malahide to 'leet' money, an annual payment from each tenant, which in 1640 amounted to two shillings.[50] The court leet dealt with petty offences, was responsible for ensuring that bread and ale were produced to a sufficient standard and that short measures were not sold.[51] The manor court of Malahide certainly had the means to punish offenders for the manor possessed a prison and stocks but nothing survives to illustrate the types of misdemeanours that were tried before it.[52] The court baron was an integral part of the manor, administering the regulations set down as the customs of the manor. It dealt with debts, trespass, disputes between tenants, and the surrender and admission to customary lands. The only surviving record of a Talbot court baron concerns the appearance in the manor court of Garristown in 1612 of Walter Dermott and his wife Ricea Longe, seeking admission to the freehold of Ricea's late father.[53] A jury of fourteen was empanelled before the seneschal, Clement FitzGerald, who admitted the Dermotts on payment of a fine of 2s. 6d., an annual chief rent of 3d. and on their swearing fealty. Despite the paucity of evidence, the inquisition *post-mortem* of Richard Talbot in 1640 and Talbot submissions to the court of claims in 1663 clearly imply that a court baron functioned almost continuously throughout the seventeenth century at Malahide.[54]

The evidence relating to tenurial practice in Malahide in the seventeenth century is no more substantial than that which pertained to the operation of the manor courts. The estate papers contain no leases on Malahide from the sixteenth through to the early eighteenth centuries. A lease perfected on the Garristown estate in 1614 by John Talbot's father, Richard, taken in conjunction with the evidence from a chancery suit in 1708 may, by analogy, shed some light on the conditions of tenure which existed in Malahide. The Garristown lessee, Richard Mahowne, was granted a term lease of twenty-one years and in addition to rent was obliged to tender annually 'one couple of wach hens out of his own house and one couple out of every tenant's house now built or hereafter built on the premises and a heriot from himself and each of his tenants on their death'.[55] The lessee was also required to maintain the building stiff, staunch and tenantable and set six good young ashes yearly. Leases for twenty-one years are referred to in the chancery suit of 1708, again in relation to Garristown, by the steward, Richard Todderick of Malahide, who was apparently reading from a rent roll.[56] In the same suit reference is made to leases on land in Malahide.[57] Despite the evidential lacuna, the indications from either end of the seventeenth century suggest that the granting of term leases was a consistent feature of tenurial practice on the Talbot estates in the 1600s. While some of the land on the manor of Garristown was held as of fee (freehold), the land sought by the Dermotts being a case in point, there is no evidence, such as chief rents, among the estate papers to suggest that Malahide contained any freehold land. As for the inhabitants of the town, one can only conjecture that they held their houses and messuages either by customary inheritance, or as tenants at will, dependent entirely upon the goodwill of the lord. Whatever their status, all tenants would have been required to grind their corn in the lord's tidemill at the mouth of the Gaybrook and to pay mulcture for the privilege.[58]

While the data produced by the Civil Survey commissioners was arrived at by estimation, and therefore cannot be employed without caution, nonetheless it can be said that Malahide's high estimated annual rental value is indicative of the key role that agriculture played in the economic life of the manor. The pattern of land use in seventeenth century Malahide was typical of the pattern which dominated agriculture throughout north county Dublin. The Civil Survey returns for the baronies which comprised Fingal suggest that a system of mixed agriculture with an overwhelming bias towards arable farming was practised. [59] The land was farmed in rotation, exhausted tillage land being taken out of production and set to pasture or meadow.[60] The Civil Survey, for example, notes that Malahide's estimated 500 acres was subdivided into 400 acres arable, 70 acres pasture and 30 acres meadow. An inquisition into the extent of the possessions of St. Mary's Abbey at Robbockeswall (Robswall), a townland contiguous to the manor of Malahide, contains details of a lease with provisos which stipulate that 'where any parte of the land in tyllage be worne out of corne to let the same to leys for pasture, and to put for the same so muche or such parcell of the said leys and furres [furze] in tillage'.[61] Talbot property in Garristown included a parcel of thirty-five acres in the townland of Baldwinstown known as Lealands and a field name, the Long Leyer, mentioned in the 1708 chancery suit, appears to confirm this practice for Malahide.[62] Thus, by rotating the land through tillage, pasture and meadow, land currently set to tillage was maintained at optimum condition. The same chancery suit reveals that it was the Talbot practice to let a farm adjoining the mansion house 'for corn instead of money' for the use of the house.[63] Corn was a generic term for cereals such as wheat, barley, and oats, all of which were grown in Malahide.[64]

If Malahide could be described as something of an agricultural jewel in the Fingal area, its maritime location also ensured that the fishing industry made a significant contribution to the economic life of the town throughout the later middle ages and into the seventeenth century. In addition to supplementing the villagers diet, it also ensured a steady flow of coinage into the local community through export to the towns of the west coast of Britain and through sale on the Dublin markets. The port-books of Chester record the landing of herring by Richard de Newton and Thomas Rede of Malahide in January 1405 and of herring and whitefish by the men of Malahide in April

of the same year.[65] De Courcy Ireland notes that many of the Irish ships landing fish at Chester, including some from Malahide in September 1405, carried
salt for the preservation of fish on their homeward journey.[66] Thus the inventory of goods appended to the 1474 will of the Malahide fisherman, John
Mold, contains a reference to '4 crannocs of salt worth 13s.4d'.[67] Chester,
however, was but one of the ports visited by Malahide fishermen. Mold's
schedule of debts notes that 'he owes John Baly of Bristol, 2s 9d. Item, he owes
Robert Oholdernys of Conway 12s. Item, to Margaret Brydall of Conway 2s.'.
The fishermen appear to have been equally as comfortable on land as at sea.
Mold, for example, double-jobbed as a farmer, for listed among his possessions
were 'five couples of wheat, barley and oats, worth 5s. Item, he has 4 hogs
worth 4s. Item, ten sheep worth 3s.4d. Item, he has one foal worth 6s.8d. Item,
in saltpetre [for the preservation of meat] six crannocs worth 16s.'. This blur-
ring of occupational lines was not solely the prerogative of fishermen. A lease
granted to William and Johanna Broun in 1496 contains a proviso safeguard-
ing the Talbot entitlement to customs should 'they [the Brouns] have any boat
going to sea'.[68] Tenant farmers, those who derived their chief income from
the land, were, apparently, in a position to augment that income by putting to
sea just as tenant fishermen, such as John Mold, were likely to turn their hands
to tillage and stock-raising. In a pre-industrialised society heavily dependent
on agriculture and prone to harvest failure, as Ireland was in the early 1640s
and 1650s, Malahide's fishing trade was an indemnity against agricultural
crises.[69] It also proved to be an indemnity against despoliation.

The fact that Malahide emerged unscathed from the 1641 rebellion is directly attributable to its importance as a supplier of fish to the Dublin city
markets. Whilst quartering at Malahide in March 1642, Ormonde suggested
to the lords justice in Dublin, contrary to their instructions that he should raze
the villages and towns of Fingal, that he forego burning 'the fisher towns upon
this coast in regard … ye market at Dublin may be prejudiced thereby'.[70]
Ormonde's appeal to self-interest clearly registered with the Council for, in
replying, they borrow Ormonde's own words: '[as the] burning of the fishers
houses may prejudice the market at Dublin we think fit your Lordship should
forbear burning them'.[71] Clearly then, the contribution of the Malahide fishermen to the city was substantial enough to warrant clemency.

The fishing industry also contributed significantly to the wealth of the
manor through customs and tithes. Edward IV's grant of the customs and admiralty of the port to Thomas Talbot in 1475 contains a schedule of tolls
payable on goods entering the haven.[72] Tolls payable on fish landed at
Malahide included:

| | |
|---|---|
| 20 large fish | 1/2d. |
| Every load of seafish | 1/2d. |

| 100 large freshwater eels | 1d. |
| Every salmon | 1/4d. |
| Every lamprey | 1/2d. |
| Every load or mease of herrings | 1/2d. |

The Talbot right to customs subsequently found its way into leases. In the case of the Brouns, cited above, the full proviso in their lease states that 'if they have any boat going to sea, they are to pay custom but no other duties'.[73] The charter of grant defines the customs and admiralty zone of jurisdiction as 'the whole of the sea coast and arm of the sea there ... from Moldowne as far as the watermill of the afforesaid Thomas [Talbot]', a distance of about two miles which corresponded to the maritime boundary of the manor.[74] In 1623 Richard Talbot extended his control over the entire estuary by acquiring the fishing rights for a further two miles beyond the watermill as far as the mouth of the Broadmeadow river from his cousin, Christopher Russell of Seatown.[75]

In 1538 the dean and chapter of St. Patrick's cathedral farmed the ecclesiastical tithes of Malahide parish to Robert Jans of Dublin. Not least among the attractions for Jans was an entitlement under the lease to 'teythe fyshe bothe grete and smalle taken ... wythyn the hawyn[haven] other w[i]thowte'.[76] In 1559 the tithes, 'as well predial [agricultural] as all personal offerings', were farmed for fifty-nine years to William Talbot of Malahide and by 1630, according to Archbishop Bulkeley, they were in the possession of Richard Talbot and generating the sum of £120.[77] The oyster fishery at the foot of the village constituted one of the appurtenances of the manor and the evidence of leases perfected in the following centuries show that the Talbots leased the oysterbeds as they would a parcel of land, the lease typically including provision for a supply of oysters to the manor house in addition to an annual rent.[78] The harvesting of the oyster fishery appears to have been regulated to ensure that it remained a self-renewing resource until as late as 1740 when, through the neglect of a lessee, the beds were ruined and had to be re-stocked with imported immature oysters from Colchester.[79]

While payments such as customs duty, tithes and rent for the messuages they occupied on manor land illustrate the economic relationship which existed between the fishermen of Malahide and the Talbot lordship, the fishermen tenants were also bound to their manorial lord through homage and fealty. On the 15 March 1642, with the imminent arrival of Ormonde's army in Malahide, the fishermen demonstrated their fidelity by carrying the Talbot family to the temporary safety of Lambay island.[80] That John Talbot expected such loyalty is clear from his petition for restoration in November 1660. In that petition he recalls how, in 1652, with the parliamentary forces in the ascendant, Dean John King, the king's envoy to the marquis of Clanricarde, sought his aid to escape out of Ireland to the Isle of Man, 'which your petitioner accordingly gave order to *his* [my italics] fishermen to doe'.[81] A further testament to the fidelity

of the fishermen to their lord is the fact that while Talbot suffered imprisonment as a consequence of his assistance to King, he was later released because
none could be found to offer evidence against him: 'no direct proof appearing that this petitioner gave order to his fishermen to convey the said Deane
as aforesaid, he was after long imprisonment released'.[82]

Observations appended to the Civil Survey returns relating to land tenure
demonstrate the commitment of the Old English gentry of Fingal to the per-
petuation of their estates in name, blood and line. Of the 484 landholdings
which comprised the baronies of Coolock, Nethercross and Balrothery, only
nine were held by purchase. The vast bulk of property devolved through inheritance. As the chief wealth of a family derived from the land they held,
great care was taken to ensure that the property rights of future generations
were safeguarded. The legal mechanism by which this was achieved was a
conveyance known as the use, the primary purpose of which was to evade tax,
specifically the crown entitlement to relief, wardship and marriage. By enfee-
offing, or granting, an estate to a number of family intimates or relatives to the
use of the grantor and his heirs, the grantor was no longer considered to be
legally seised of the land. Since he was no longer seised of any property, the
crown had no claim on the estate upon his death. Failure to perfect a conveyance to use resulted in the exaction of relief and the sale of the wardship
and marriage to the highest bidder who was effectively given licence to asset-
strip the estate for the duration of the wardship. More significantly, given the
volatile circumstances of the sixteenth and early seventeenth centuries, since
the beneficiary of a conveyance to use was no longer seised of the property, the
estate could not be forfeited as a consequence of his treason. At the Restoration
of Charles II conveyances to use perfected before the 1641 rebellion were to
prove invaluable in securing for some innocent heirs an interest in the estates
of nocent fathers.

The wardship of Richard Talbot fell prey to the crown in 1596 upon the
death of his grandfather, William. Fortunately, his uncle, Sir John Talbot, who had
claims on the crown owing to his service during the Nine Years War, preserved
the estate by purchasing the wardship from Queen Elizabeth for £300.[83]
Some indication of the lucrative benefits which accrued from the possession
of the wardship and marriage of a minor can be ascertained by the fact that
Sir John's stewardship of the estate earned him £800 on Richard's marriage
and £2,000 in profits from the land, money which would have benefited the
heir if a conveyance to use had been properly executed.[84] Even though the
wardship was in the hands of a close relative, and hence might be considered
relatively secure from depredation, the sequel was bitter and fought over in a
Chancery suit around 1608.[85] While Sir John appears to have left the estate in
good order, he fell out with his nephew over sums of money he advanced in
excess of Richard's allowance, claiming they were but loans. Richard, for his
part, construed the advances as gifts and reckoned Sir John had been more

than amply compensated from the profits of the estate. The bitterness generated by the wardship explains the care which Richard Talbot took, when he
came of age, to create a family settlement by a conveyance to use that would be
impervious to challenge. Having been educated to law at Trinity College as a
ward and subsequently at Gray's Inn in London, he was more than competent
to ensure as much.[86] In 1619 he enfeoffed Malahide, Garristown and Castlering
to his own use and to the use of his heirs.[87] As the Irish Statute of Uses (1634)
placed seisin in the hands of the person in whose favour the uses were created
it thus nullifying the beneficial tax evasion element of the conveyance to use,
Talbot circumvented the statute to achieve the same effect by amending his
deed of feeoffment in July 1640 to create a trust for the term of ninety-nine
years to provide for his wife's dowry, annuities for his non-preferred sons and
a portion for his daughter Jane.[88] At the same time he also entailed the estate
for life to his son, John, with remainder to his heirs male. The real value of this
conveyance was to emerge in the 1660s when the Talbots attempted to retrieve their forfeited estate.

   Feeoffees, those to whom the estate was entrusted by the conveyance to
use, were carefully selected. They were certainly close friends and relatives
who could be depended upon to shepherd the estate conscientiously according
to the wishes of the conveyor. Notably, with the exception of Thomas Hanlon,
the feeoffees of the 1619 conveyance and the amended conveyance of 1640
were all representatives of Old English Catholic families of the Pale. James
Bath of Drumcondra, Robert Cheevers of Connaughton and the lawyer
Richard Berford of Ballabyne were feeoffees to both conveyances, an indication of the esteem in which they were held by the Talbots. Cheevers were also
related to the Talbots through marriage, as was James Plunkett of Longwood,
county Meath, who was enfeoffed in the 1619 conveyance. Nicholas Canny
claims that the greatest contribution of Old English lawyers, such as Richard
Talbot and Richard Berford, was in employing their knowledge of the laws of
conveyance to enable the Old English Catholics to survive 'as a social, if not a
political, elite into the seventeenth century'.[89] Conveyances to use, then, linked
the Talbots into a network of mutual interest among the Old English Catholic
community, a network, as we shall see, which was extended and consolidated by
the Talbots through marriage and through joint action in defence of the Pale.

   Richard Stanihurst's claim that 'the Anglo-Irish have cut themselves off so
completely from the old Irish that the humblest of the colonists in the English
Pale would not give his daughter in marriage to the noblest Irish lord' would
appear, by even the most cursory analysis, to be only partially accurate.[90]
'Marcher' lords of the Pale, such as the Fitzgeralds of Kildare, by force of geographical circumstances, appear to have contracted pragmatic marriage alliances
with native Irish families, the marriage of Eleanor Fitzgerald to Manus O'
Donnell in the early sixteenth century being a case in point.[91] The Talbots of
Malahide, whose principal seat was situated comfortably in the heart of the

*Table 3: Marriage alliances of the Talbots of Malahide, 1500–1800*
(Key; d: daughter, m.: married, unm.: unmarried )[92]

---

*Sir Peter* m. (i) Catherine FitzGerald (d. Earl of Kildare)
(ii) Janet Eustace (Confey)

*Thomas* m. Katherine Betagh (Moynalty)

*William* m. Mary Bermingham (d. Lord Chief Justice
Patrick Bermingham)

*Patrick* m. Katherine Cheevers (Maceston) c. 1584
John m. Bridget Talbot (d. Sir John Talbot of Grafton , England)
Alice m. John Finglas (Tipersoule)
Anne m. William Wogan (Rathcoffey)
Jenet m. Robert Barnewall (Dunbroe)
Elizabeth m. Christopher Russell (Seatown)

*Richard* m. Elizabeth Kempe (Sussex) c. 1607

*John* m. Katherine Plunkett (d. Earl of Fingall) 1639
Elizabeth m. John Draycott (Mornington) 1639–40

*Richard* m. Frances Talbot (Carton) c.1670

*Richard* (unm. )   John m. Frances Wogan (Rathcoffey) 1735
Valentine m. Mary Tobin (no issue)
Mary m. Robert Dillon Ann Elizabeth    Frances m. Robert Carroll

*Richard* (son of John) m. Margaret O' Reilly (Ballinlough) 1765

*Richard Wogan* Talbot m. Catherine Mapas (Rochestown)
James m. Anne Rodberd (Somerset)
John m. Julia Arundel (d. Lord Arundel and Wardour)
Barbara m. Sir Wm. Young
Frances Catherine m. Lt. Gen. Sir George Airey
Elizabeth m. Capt. George Mellifont 1796
Charlotte m. Mervin Cutliffe (Devon) 1805

---

Pale, had little necessity and, apparently, even less inclination, to forge alliances
with the native Irish. They preserved their ethnic distinctiveness, perpetuated
their name and shepherded the inheritance rights of their children by marry-

ing exclusively within their own ethnic group. Table 3, a genealogy of Talbot marriage alliances contracted between the 1500 and 1800, confirms this bias, the marriage partners until the later eighteenth century emerging almost exclusively from the most prominent Old English Catholic families of the Pale, the exceptions being the unions contracted with the English Catholic families, the Kempes of Sussex and the Talbots of Grafton. A prejudice against intermarriage with the native Irish persisted in the family right into the eighteenth century. When Richard Talbot the younger, heir apparent to the lordship, married Margaret O'Reilly of Ballinlough, county Westmeath, in 1765, his uncle Richard was reported to have been 'not much pleased at his nephew's marriage into a family of poor Irish blood and name, the first of the kind that had ever taken place in that of Malahide'.[93]

Three marriages merit particular attention because of their relevance to the history of the Talbots in the seventeenth century. The marriage in the late 1500s of John Talbot (later Sir John) to Bridget Talbot, the daughter of Sir John Talbot of Grafton, re-established links with the Talbots, earls of Shrewsbury, of whom the Malahide Talbots were an offshoot. When the Shrewsbury male line failed in the early seventeenth century, the Grafton Talbots emerged as heirs to the earldom and were prominent in the Stuart court at the Restoration. This connection should have been invaluable to the Talbots of Malahide in their efforts to retrieve their estate but, perhaps because of residual bitterness dating from the Chancery suit, I could find no evidence to indicate that they ever employed their influence at court in support of their Malahide kin. The marriage in 1637 of John Talbot, lord of Malahide from 1640, to Catherine Plunkett was a prestigious and powerful connection. Catherine's father, Luke, was the first earl of Fingall and her uncle was the lawyer Nicholas Plunkett, a prominent Confederate during the rebellion and later an agent at the royal court for dispossessed Old English Catholic families. Richard Talbot's marriage in 1670 to Frances Talbot, daughter of Sir Robert Talbot of Carton, represented a continuation of the close ties that had always existed between the Talbots of Malahide and the cadet branch of the family at Carton. Frances was niece to Richard Talbot (later earl of Tyrconnell). Richard of Carton's close relationship with James, duke of York, enabled him to wield considerable influence in Whitehall and where influence failed he did not scruple to bribe.[94]

Endogamous marriage alliances were contracted not solely to ensure *limpieza de sangre*, a purity in the blood line, they were also part of the defensive mechanism of a colony that was physically under siege. Like enfeeoffment to use, endogamy knitted the Old English community together, creating a community of interest and a sense of solidarity in the face of the sole sixteenth and early seventeenth century military threat to the integrity of their estates and families, the native Irish. The Talbots, semi-marcher lords through their landholding in Castlering, county Louth, had direct experience of that threat. William Talbot was lord of Malahide in 1554 when Malahide Court was attacked by the O'Byrnes and O'Tooles, an assault that almost carried the castle, and throughout the later sixteenth century he was summoned repeatedly to the county Dublin 'hostings' to protect the county against the Ulster rebels.[95] His son, John Talbot, raised a company of soldiers at his own expense to serve against the Ulster rebels during the Nine Years War and was knighted after the battle of the Blackwater. It is not surprising, therefore, that an antipathy to the native Irish, founded on the belief that they were despoilers, should become entrenched in the Talbot mentality. In his will of 1596, William stipulated the payment of £15 to his grandson, Richard Talbot, from his lands in county Louth, with a proviso that the sum need not be paid 'if the said manor, lands, tenements and hereditaments in the countie of Louthe ... shall come to be waste by the incursions or bad neighbourhood of the Irish herein or their confederates or adherents'. [96] Talbot's concern in this regard were well-founded for shortly before his death Castlering was indeed 'wasted by the incursions of the rebels'.[97] A prejudice against intermarriage with the native Irish did not imply that natives were unwelcome in the Old English enclave. The jury empanelled in the manor court of Garristown in 1612, for example, contains the names of two native Irish, Richard Don (Brown-haired) Macan and William Bane (Fair-haired) Macan, both Talbot tenants and, as we have seen, the ethnic composition of the town of Malahide was evenly divided between those of Old English and of native Irish origin.[98]

Throughout the sixteenth and early seventeenth centuries, and even during the 1640s, the Talbots of Malahide remained unshakeably loyal to the crown. William Talbot, as we have seen, was regularly commissioned to muster the Pale forces during the later sixteenth century and Sir John Talbot served the crown during the Nine Years War. The activities of John Talbot from the outbreak of the rebellion in 1641, which will be examined below, were an elaboration of that traditional loyalty. The Talbots were pragmatic enough to realise, in the first instance, that the title to their estate derived from and was secured by the crown. A secure title, in the form of letters patent from the crown, was, as their own experience demonstrated, a guarantee against predators. In 1482 they successfully withstood a challenge from the city of Dublin to their entitlement to the customs of the port.[99] Yet again, in 1639, when the attorney-general, Sir Richard Osbaldeston, brought an action for the king against Richard Talbot, maintaining that Talbot had 'for a number of years used and claimed to have and use without any warrant or royal grant the office of admiralty in the manor of Malahide, and the power of holding a court of admiralty there, and to enjoy the profits without accounting to the king', Richard Talbot was able to plead letters patent of 8 March 1475 and have his right upheld. [100] The *quid pro quo* for such guarantees was, of course, continued loyalty to the crown. The confiscations that followed the Geraldine revolt in Munster and that of the O'Neills and O'Donnells in Ulster were salutary warnings of the consequences of open rebellion. Even within the seventeenth century Pale the memory of the confiscations which followed the Kildare (1534) and Baltinglass (1580) revolts was a reminder of the dangers of mani-festing disaffection in arms. John Burnell, a near neighbour of the Talbots, was executed for complicity in the Kildare revolt and his family estate at Balgriffin was forfeited in 1545.[101] It was, undoubtedly, their awareness of the momen-tous nature of rebellion that influenced the Catholic gentry of the Pale to de-fect to the Irish rebels in 1641 only after they had first satisfied themselves as to the *bona fide* royalist sympathies of the rebels.

If Talbot politics were national, their religious beliefs were decidedly do-mestic. Their dogged adherence to Catholicism during the 1600s, when con-formity to the established church promised significant economic and political advantage, suggests that their religious belief was the product of deep convic-tion. Denied access to the parish church adjoining Malahide Court, which had been sequestered after the Reformation to Protestant use, they accom-modated Catholic worship in the manor house. In 1630 Archbishop Bulkeley noted of Malahide that 'all the parishioners are recusants and goe to mass at Mr. Talbot of Malahide's house more usually than heretofore'.[102] Like many other leading Catholic families within the Pale, a younger son, George, was ordained to the Catholic priesthood and it was probably his presence at the manor house in 1630 which contributed to the increase in mass-going noted by Bulkeley.[103] A distinctive feature of local religious devotion was the extra-ordinary reverence accorded to the Blessed Virgin, evidence of which is to be found in the testaments and iconography of fifteenth through seventeenth century Malahide. The fisherman, John Mold, for example, commences his 1474 will by bequeathing his soul 'to Almighty God the Blessed Virgin and all the saints'.[104] In the nave of the medieval parish church the effigy tomb of Maude Plunkett (died 1482), a Talbot widow, bears a shield which portrays saltire, two swords piercing a heart, symbolic of the Virgin Mary. [105] The church of Garristown was dedicated to the Blessed Virgin (that of Malahide contin-ued in the name of St. Fenweis, the founder of a pre-Norman church on that site). In the town of Malahide the annual pattern was held on 15 August, the feast of the Assumption of the Blessed Virgin, at the Lady well, within which a statue of the Virgin was displayed on a shelf beneath the canopy.[106]

Marian veneration, as we have noted in relation to the Plunkett effigy tomb, was not confined to the lower orders of Malahide society for the Catholicism of the Talbot family was highly-coloured by their own particular allegiance to the Blessed Virgin. Emblematic of this devotion was the carved figure of the Assumption which hung over the fireplace in the Oak Room at Malahide Court (figure 7). A curious, much faded document, a rhapsody on the statue written in a late seventeenth or early eighteenth century hand by a grandson of John Talbot, sheds considerable light on the significance of the Virgin to the family.[107] The icon, according to the writer, was hung over the fireplace in imitation of the great Old Testament figures who 'placed seraphims and cherubs up in there domesticks to praise God ... before saints was in heaven'. The writer's father told him that:

> 'the image of our blessed lady was put up which he saide none in Ireland had it over the chimney but our house which he saide she being the mother of ye family placed over ye chimney covers all her children under her mantel and asuming into heaven carries them along with her and protects them in ye surest and warmest place nourishes them like ye henn under her wings as mother of all people'.

Reflecting, perhaps, the effects of the counter-Reformation in projecting the image of Christ to the fore, the writer continues, 'In ye Church shee is in a sorte of parradice there our Saviour ascension was over the doore to shew none can enter there without entring under him to glorie'. While acknowledging the pre-eminence of Christ within the church, the writer nevertheless stresses the Talbot belief in the intercessionary role of the Virgin when he writes that 'she as mother is placed before ye doore to shew whoever enters must kneele for her blessing'.

The evidence in the rhapsody suggests that the Talbots joined with the townspeople in celebrating the Malahide pattern and also made an annual pilgrimage to St. Marnock's well in nearby Portmarnock: 'I myself am a witness and goe often to St. Marnock's with my parents. I asked them the raison of goeing to ye well and ... but ye parish why not our Lady [well in Malahide] they said they went to our Lady too'. The tradition of pilgrimage to St. Marnock's well, which persisted into the late eighteenth century, originated, according to the rhapsody, in the appearance of the Virgin to an heirless ancestor praying before the statue in the Oak Room.[108] She commanded him to 'goe there because this was the place of blood conquerd by God first and soe vowed to God and must be performed to [Him] a sacrifice in memory of his conquest never to be blotted of posterity'. The 'place of blood' suggests that the well in Portmarnock was the place where the first Talbot colonists expelled the remnants of Hamond MacTorkill's Norse settlement in the area, shortly after MacTorkill's death in Dublin in 1172. The Talbots subsequently granted away this land 'in honour of God and of the Blessed Virgin' to the Cistercians, who held land nearby and whose monastery on the north bank of the River Liffey was St. Mary's Abbey.[109] The Marian command, then, however it is construed in a religious sense, clearly reflects an attempt to preserve the memory of that infant colony by imposing the obligation of pilgrimage. That the Talbots considered themselves bound in duty to fulfil this obligation is clear from the actions of John Talbot in the mid-1650s. Transplanted to Connacht and with no habitation or land assigned to him, he appealed to the Commonwealth in April 1655 for a safe-conduct pass to return to Malahide to attend to the sale of his corn and other goods. The disposal of his goods, however, was partly a pretext for a pilgrimage to St. Marnock's. The rhapsody recalls that 'when he

7. Chimney-piece of the assumption of the Blessed Virgin in
the Oak Room, Malahide Castle.

was transplanted to Conaugh he was to come up to doe the pilgrimage att St.
Marnocks ... he desired to keep puntually the pilgrimage and ... saide on his
blessing "you will never have anny blessing if you doe not observe her co-
mand"'. The mystique surrounding the oak carving is recalled in local folk-
lore in the legend of its disappearance during Miles Corbet's seven year
usurpation of Malahide Court and its miraculous re-appearance after he had
fled.[110] While the Talbots themselves never gave credence to the story, the
essence of the legend, that the Virgin found the puritan Corbet's presence odi-

ous, does convey the sense of abhorrence with which the local inhabitants viewed him.[111] Corbet's flight and execution in 1662 and the resumption of the Talbot lordship in the 1660s, then, were converted by the legend, into a paradigm of the manifestations of the Blessed Virgin in the real world, bestowing her favour and presence on the good and faithful and shunning the heretic. Given the way in which the cult of the Virgin suffused the religious landscape of Malahide it is not surprising that the Talbots had little difficulty in reconciling allegiance to the crown from which temporal title to the land derived, with devotion to the Blessed Virgin to whom they credited their accession to and continued occupation of Malahide.

This chapter has attempted to sketch the cultural background which shaped the response of John Talbot to the setbacks he encountered in the decades which followed his accession to the lordship. As we have seen, Talbot's inheritance was not simply a question of accession to a few thousand acres. It included a network of connections within the Old English community of the Pale which had been forged through kinship, strategic marriage alliances, cooperation in defence of the Pale and participation in conveyances to use. Within the manor itself, the tenants, as we saw in the case of the Dermotts in Garristown, were bound by fealty to their lord. That this involved more than a hollow ritual is evident in the response of the Malahide fishermen to the approach of Ormonde's army in 1642 and to Talbot's order that they should transport Dean King to the Isle of Man in 1652. In turn, Talbot's assistance to Dean King was a demonstration of his fealty to the crown, a statement of his political loyalty. As a complement to this social, cultural, political and legal capital, John Talbot inherited one of the most profitable estates in Fingal. In addition to rental payments, the wealth of the lordship was augmented by a whole range of duties such as tithes, the port customs, the manorial dues of 'leet' money, entry fines and mulcture. At a personal level, the Talbot Marian tradition imbued John Talbot with a deep religious conviction which emerged most notably during the mid-1650s when the family was all but destitute in Connacht. Talbot's inheritance, then, comprised realty but also a complex set of connections, relationships and values. In that respect, Talbot faced into the lean years not as a blank slate on which fortune could inscribe what it would, but equipped with a broad range of resources which could be drawn on and developed as circumstances required.

# War and Transplantation 1641–1659

When John Talbot assumed the lordship of Malahide, Garristown and Castlering in July 1640, he could not have foreseen that within little more than a year he would find himself embroiled in a struggle for survival that would endure for the rest of his life. By the time of his death in 1671, he would suffer outlawry, imprisonment, the sequestration of his estate, transplantation and partial restoration and the fabric of the society in which he dwelt would be irrevocably transformed. The event which precipitated a downward spiral in Talbot fortunes was the outbreak of rebellion in Ulster in October, 1641. While an analysis of the complexity of the events which provoked the Ulster rebellion and the defection of the Old English to the rebel camp is beyond the scope of this study, the activities of the Catholic gentry of Fingal during the winter and spring of 1641–2, when they took the field against the lords justice in Dublin, merit close attention. It was this brief period of rebellion which was to shape the history of John Talbot and Malahide for the following three decades.

Fingal was initially slow to embrace the rebellion. While counties Louth and Meath fell to the rebels in October and the Old English gentry there were heavily engaged within a month, Fingal remained calm until early December.[1] Hence, when Sergeant-Major Roper and Sir Patrick Wemys led a contingent of 600 poorly trained soldiers and a troop of horsemen out of Dublin on 27 November to assist the besieged garrison at Drogheda, they passed completely unhindered through Fingal.[2] On the morning of 29 November, however, they were overwhelmed by the Irish rebels at Julianstown just beyond the county Dublin border.[3] A rebel victory so close to the capital city appears to have resolved the ambivalence with which the gentry of Fingal had viewed the rebellion. The lords justice, whose reluctance to arm the Old English adequately in November had left them exposed to the rebels, took fright at the unexpected success of the rebels and now sought to employ them to gain time while they awaited aid from England. On 3 December they directed letters to the nobility nearest them, inviting them to Dublin to confer with them concerning the safety of the kingdom.[4] With a degree of equivocation, however, that was to characterise their communications with the Old English of the Pale throughout December, a party of soldiers was sent out on the same day to detain some pillagers who had ransacked a Protestant house at the Baskin, near Kinsealy, and finding some strangers lodged at an inn at Santry, murdered them and carried their heads back to Dublin in triumph.[5] The rebel victory at Julianstown, however, appears to have been of critical significance. While the letters of the lords justice were being dispatched, the chief lords of the Pale, Gormanstown, Fingall, Slane, Trimleston, Dunsany, Louth and Netterville, together with a host of other gentry, were compacting with the rebels at Crofty, near Tara.[6]

On 4 December, Netterville's son, Luke, who had been present at Crofty, issued a proclamation in the towns of Fingal summoning a general meeting at Swords for the eighth, the day appointed by the lords justice for the Old English to come to Dublin.[7] The purpose of this meeting was to organise for the defence of the north county against the lords justice in Dublin and a crowd of about 1,200 assembled. On the balance of available evidence it appears unlikely that John Talbot of Malahide attended this gathering or if so, that he determined against committing himself. Having but recently acceded to his father's estate, Talbot may have thought it prudent to avoid an association which might jeopardise his inheritance. As a leading proprietor in the region, his presence would not easily have escaped the attention of the lords justice, who appear to have had immediate intelligence of the assembly, and when, on 9 December, they summoned the principal gentry involved to Dublin to account for the rising out, his name does not appear on the summons.[8] The 1641–52 county Dublin depositions which document outrages and pillaging during that period contain no reference to Talbot and advance no evidence to suggest that Malahide remained anything but tranquil until March 1642 when Malahide Court was garrisoned by Ormonde.[9] Furthermore, while observations appended to the schedule of proprietors in the books of the Civil Survey (1654–56) provide details of the rebellious activities of many Old English proprietors during the 1640s, no such attribution is made to Talbot. Despite maintaining an apparently innocent demeanour in the early months of the rebellion, Talbot was nevertheless indicted for treason before the king's bench and outlawed in early February 1642.[10] As an outlaw, Talbot was immediately deprived of the protection of the law, disabled from bringing a court action for redress and his estate became liable for sequestration.

The principals at Swords having failed to appear before the lords justice on 8 December, a warrant was issued from Dublin ordering the assembly to disperse and requiring the Fingallian leaders to attend the Council on the tenth.[11] The Old English refused to comply with either instruction, citing the murder of the four Catholics at Santry as the occasion of their assembly, maintaining that they were 'being dayly put into many feares by certaine intelligence given of unexpected attempts against our lives' and asserting their unwillingness to appear before the lords until they were 'some certaine way assured by your Lordships of the safety of our lives before wee runn the hazard thereof'.[12] The lords poured scorn on the fears of the Fingallian gentry and ordered them to appear on the seventeenth.[13] Whether or not the leaders of the Swords army would have attended the Council on that date quickly became irrelevant. On 11 December a band of pillagers from Raheny descended on a ship lying aground near Clontarf and proceeded to strip it bare. Although the lords justice were quickly aware of the identity of the pillagers from a deposition taken on the fourteenth by John Temple, master of the rolls and a member of the Council, a party of soldiers led by Sir Charles Coote came out from Dublin on the following day and burnt and looted the fishing village of Clontarf, taking particular pains to destroy the house of George King, one of the gentry assembled at Swords.[14] On 22 December Coote burned the villages of Santry and Finglas and after a brief skirmish with the Fingallian army returned to the city.[15] That the lords justice intended these acts as a direct provocation is clear from their letter to the earl of Leicester, the lord lieutenant, written before Coote emerged from Dublin. Referring to the pillaged ship at Clontarf, which had now become 'several barks', they wrote: 'and if to revenge this villainy on the fishermen of Clontarf and thereabouts so near us we send forth a party of soldiers to burn and spoil those rebels' houses and corn, the gentlemen of the Pale will immediately take new offence, but that we will adventure upon, for now there is no dalliance with them who so far declare themselves against the state, not caring what scorns are put upon the Government, wherein it is observable that the landlord of Clontarf [George King] is one of the gentlemen risen in arms at Swords'.[16] The Pale gentry did take offence at the attack on King's house, they fixated upon it and cited it frequently thereafter in their complaints against the lords justice. Coote followed up his earlier sallies by comprehensively routing Netterville's largely peasant army at Swords on New Year's Eve, pushing the Old English further back from the city.[17] It was early March 1642 before Ormonde succeeded in clearing north county Dublin of rebels and in the interim the writs of outlawry issued like confetti from the king's bench. Any prospect of submitting to the lords justice at this point were dampened by the jailing and racking of a number of Old English gentry who took advantage of Ormonde's proximity to submit themselves to his protection.[18]

If Talbot was not actively involved in the rebellion, however, it raises the question as to how he should find himself outlawed. In the rush to attaint as many Catholics as possible in the opening weeks of the rising, subtleties such as the presence of a number of people bearing the same name may have eluded those processing the writs. Ominously for Talbot of Malahide, his kinsman John Talbot of Robertstown, county Meath, who also held land to the west and south of Malahide, was one of the principals involved in Netterville's army. He appended his name to the communications which issued from that camp and was one of those summoned to answer to the lords justices.[19] After the defeat at Swords he submitted to Ormonde and was jailed in Dublin for over a year.[20] John Talbot of Belgard, another relative, was later charged with robbery and murder.[21] The Talbots of Carton, county Kildare, Gerald, Gilbert and Garrett, were also indicted at the same time and Robert Talbot, baronet, later emerged as a leading figure in the Confederate administration at Kilkenny.[22] The Talbot name was therefore prominently associated with the defecting gentry. Evidence from the court of claims in 1663 suggests that Talbot of Malahide's younger brother, Richard, may have played an active military role in Netterville's army.[23] In this he would have been following the precedent set in November in county Louth, where the rebellion was first embraced by junior members of Old English families, a cautious practice which placed family estates at one remove from sequestration should the venture fail.[24] When Richard's claim for a rentcharge of £40 per annum bequeathed him by his father came before the court of claims in March 1663 the claim was not entered and the case not heard.[25] The following month John Talbot's son, also Richard, pressed his claim to be adjudged innocent and to be restored to the remainder of the estate upon his father's death.[26] His claim was upheld despite evidence on oath from an Elizabeth Baines of Swords that Richard Talbot had been a captain of the rebels. To a court less accustomed to legal chicanery, Baines's evidence would have appeared astonishing, for the claimant was in his early twenties and could not have been more than two years old at the outbreak of the rebellion. It seems that the real target of her evidence may have been his uncle, who, forewarned of her presence in the court precinct, prudently decided against pressing his claim. Many indictments, in any case, appear to have been procured illicitly. Carte, for example, refers to a letter read before the Council from a person 'who claimed great merit to himself in getting some hundreds of gentlemen indicted and the rather *for that he had laid out sums of money to procure witnesses to give evidence to a jury for finding of those indictments*'.[27] In the final analysis, Talbot's mere presence within an area controlled by the rebels, as Fingal was for approximately three months, was probably all that was required to have him attainted. Paradoxically, there was no way that Talbot could have avoided some contact with the rebels for the lords justice had prohibited entry to Dublin by all but those ordered to do so by Ormonde or Coote or those bringing corn.[28] Thus, while no evidence exists to implicate John Talbot of Malahide in the rebellion, the coincidence of the involvement of his namesakes and kin, the possible participation of his brother, his presence within rebel quarters, perjury and the desire of the Council to sequester the Old English Catholic estates and to have 'honest Protestants planted in their places' probably account for one or more of the grounds on which his outlawry was based.[29] When to Talbot's outlawry were added those of his brothers, George (a Catholic priest), William and Richard, and those of the Malahide yeomen Robert Bowen of Mabestown, Thomas Jones and Luke Toole, the way was cleared for the sequestration of Malahide.[30] That prospect became a reality with the passing of the Adventurers' act in 1642 which proposed to reward all who adventured money for the suppression of the rebellion with forfeited land in Ireland.[31] The Adventurers' act was to remain suspended for a decade, awaiting only the pacification of the country for its implementation.

Ormonde's punitive sweep through the north county in February and March 1642, his defeat of the Confederate force at Kilsallaghan and the garrisoning of Finglas, Artane, Feltrim, Baldoyle, Corduff, Swords and Malahide into 1643, ensured that Fingal thereafter remained subdued within the English quarter.[32] Leading Old English gentry of Fingal, Lord Gormanstown, the Nettervilles, George King, George Blackeney, Nicholas Hollywood, Philip Hore, John Finglas and James Bath fled the county and pursued the war as members of the Confederation. John Talbot, as we have seen, escaped briefly to Lambay island ahead of Ormonde's arrival in Malahide.[33] While this act might be interpreted as the actions of a guilty man, it can be argued that it was simply an attempt to hide out until the storm had passed, for his fishermen could have as conveniently transported him to the safety of the rebel quarters had he so desired. Retrieved from Lambay by a ship sent from Howth, Talbot returned to discover that Malahide Court was to be garrisoned by 200 men.[34] As an outlaw he should have been immediately detained and jailed like Dunsany, Talbot of Robertstown, George Aylmer and the other Old English who had submitted but some form of *rapprochement* appears to have been developed with Ormonde which enabled him to evade that penalty. Ormonde certainly appears to have satisfied himself that Talbot had played no part in the war for in 1660 he joined with Sir Maurice Eustace in supporting Talbot's petition for restoration: 'We do very well know that he was faithfull and loyall to your Ma[jes]ties most royall father and lived inoffensively at Malahoyd aforesaid and did contribute to his power to the maintenance of your Ma[jes]ties army whilst the Lord Marquis of Ormond continued there [in Ireland]'.[35] Talbot's contribution to the maintenance of the army was probably initially in the form of victuals to the garrison but Ormonde's commendation suggests that he continued to supply Ormonde's forces throughout the 1640s, long after Malahide ceased to play a role in the theatre of military operations. Whether Talbot's contribution to the army was an attempt to demonstrate his royalist credentials, credits to be offset against his outlawry, is not clear. His apparent non-participation in the Fingallian revolt and risks he undertook to demonstrate that loyalty in the early 1650s, when the country was ruled by the Commonwealth, suggests that it was probably a reflex of traditional Talbot loyalty to the crown.

The lords justice, with little prescience, had instructed Ormonde to burn the countryside about Dublin to deny the rebels the advantage of provisions. The ease with which the Fingallian confederates were crushed, however, suggests that they grossly overestimated their strength and capacity and it made no logistical sense to ravage Fingal, which as 'the garner of the kingdom' was a major contributor of foodstuffs to the city.[36] By June 1642 it was apparent that there would be no seed for the following year which was 'likely to cause much famine' and soldiers were asked to desist from cutting green corn and hay and from pillaging.[37] With the removal of the immediate military threat to the city, the need to secure provisions for the citizens and particularly for the army, which was on the verge of mutiny over pay and victualling, now became a priority for the lords justice.[38] Proclamations were issued in early 1643 offering protection to anyone, including those who had been in rebellion, willing to cultivate the land about the city and fishermen were allowed to operate without hindrance.[39] Fears of a mutiny by the army persisted, however, and in March 1643 the lords justice instructed Ormonde to take part of the army into the country in order 'by the sword to gaine from the Rebells provision of victualls' and should this not be possible they suggested that he might feed the troops 'by voluntarie reliefe of victuals from some of the Rebells in respect of sparing them for a time'.[40] It was precisely this form of temporary respite that Talbot had secured from Ormonde almost a year earlier. Ormonde was not entirely well disposed towards despoliation and his treatment of the fishing towns demonstrates that he correctly anticipated the folly of such a policy. It was Talbot's good fortune that he was able to insinuate himself into the interstices between the Council's policy of despoliation and its consequences, the threat of famine or mutiny, to retain a hold on his estate.

John Talbot remained at Malahide throughout the 1640s, his contribution to Ormonde's army probably leading to a more formal, though temporary, possession by way of a custodium from the crown.[41] While this was a costly business, he was effectively paying rent to the crown in order to work his own land, it was nevertheless a far healthier situation than that which pertained to those Fingallians who had fled. In their absence, custodiums of the estates of Luke Netterville, Philip Hore, John Talbot of Robertstown and Lord Gormanstown were granted to government officials and army officers, enabling them to receive the rents and reversions from the sequestered lands and houses.[42] Talbot, by contrast, made a virtue of simply holding on. The protection offered by the proclamations and the periodic renewal of the truce agreed between the Confederates and the Dublin government in 1643 ensured that he remained relatively undisturbed throughout that decade. Talbot's period of grace extended into the early 1650s through a conjunction of circumstances. The Adventurers' act could not be implemented until the country was pacified, for few would have considered planting while the war was continuing, and recurring food shortages compelled the government to interfere as little as possible with those who were actually working the land, however guilty they were alleged to be. Thus, in time, Talbot's crown custodium was converted into a commonwealth custodium.

While these conditions persisted and insofar as he eschewed any act that might offend the Cromwellian government, his tenure was reasonably secure. In February 1652, however, having held his estate for a number of years under a veneer of 'passive obedience unto Cromwell's partie', his royalist sympathies were tested and his response to that challenge incurred severe retribution.[43] With the Parliamentary forces in the ascendant, Charles II, now at Stirling, sent an envoy, Dean John King, to the marquis of Clanricarde, Ormonde's successor as lord lieutenant.[44] King's mission was to take an account of the conditions in Ireland, in particular to determine the extent of support which remained for the royalist cause in Ireland. After many delays, King finally completed his mission but now faced the difficulty of transporting Clanricarde's letters out of the country. Talbot's loyalty to the crown was evidently widely known for according to his petition for restoration, King was recommended 'by some friends in your Majesties Army unto your petitioner [Talbot] for seeing him safely transported into the Isle of Man which your petitioner accordingly gave order to his fishermen to doe'.[45] King was spirited away to the Isle of Man in February 1652, from whence he succeeded in reaching Paris to deliver his account. Talbot was less fortunate for 'notice thereof being given to Miles Corbet and the rest of the Rump's Commissioners in Ireland he was apprehended and imprisoned and his estate of Mallahide given to the said Corbet ... he was after long imprisonment released and transported into Connacht'.[46] After Charles II's restoration he was able to quote this incident to his advantage, citing it as a manifestation of his loyalty and imposing a debt on the monarchy which was repaid by a proviso in the Act of Settlement.

Talbot's assistance to King brought him the type of exposure he had successfully shunned for over a decade and yet, ironically, he was reprieved by circumstances similar to those which enabled him to survive the 1640s. His imprisonment cannot have commenced earlier than mid-February 1652 nor continued longer than the spring of 1653 for from May of that year he was again paying rent for Malahide to the Commonwealth.[47] Talbot claimed that he was released because there was no 'direct proof appearing that [he] gave order to his fishermen to convey the said Deane [King]'.[48] It may equally have been prompted by economic expedience. As early as 1651 the country had, yet again, begun to experience serious food shortages.[49] By 1652 the situation had deteriorated and to conserve the food supply the Commonwealth commissioners prohibited the export of livestock, cereals and even the malting of oats for ale was forbidden.[50] By May 1653, the date on which Talbot's custodium was granted, the commissioners reported that there were 'great multitudes of vagrant poor, caused by the devastation of the rebellion who have acquired habits of licentiousness and idleness. Some feed on carrion and weeds and starve on the highways, poor children deserted or exposed by their parents are fed on by ravenous wolves or wild beasts and birds of prey'.[51] More importantly, the commissioners were acutely conscious of the arrears of pay owing to the army.[52] Thus, in practical terms, Talbot was far more valuable working the land and paying rent than were he to remain languishing in jail. His rent for Malahide for the year from May 1653 was £150, in addition to which he also made a 'high contribution', probably in the form of corn at a low fixed price.[53] This was a severe imposition, and particularly so when regard is had of the fact that by 1704, the combined rental for the manors of both Malahide and Garristown amounted to no more than £645.[54]

Talbot suffered a further setback when Miles Corbet, commissioner of affairs in Ireland and chief baron of the Exchequer, fleeing from an outbreak of plague in Dublin, ousted him from the manor house in December 1653. Claiming that his house and family in Dublin were 'visited by the plague and the [house] next his is also visited', he sought a lease on Talbot's premises.[55] Corbet had little difficulty in securing a seven year lease on the premises from his fellow commissioners, for, as he wrote, Talbot was 'indicted for acting in the first year of rebellion, and is to remove by the late printed instructions into Connaught'.[56] The ignominy of the loss of his home, however, can have counted for little when compared to his projected transplantation into Connacht. The 'late printed instructions' refers to a proclamation dated 14 October 1653 which ordered into Connacht before 1 May 1654, 'all persons in Ireland who have right to articles [under the Commonwealth Act of Settlement of 1652] for the better security of all those parts of Ireland which are now intended to be planted with English and Protestants'.[57] Nor could he hope to defer transplanting for any great length of time on account of food shortages. By 1654 the food crisis had apparently improved to the extent that in April of that year Talbot himself was able to petition successfully for a rent reduction 'in regard the cheepness of corne'.[58] Miles Corbet, now residing in Talbot's house, was one of the three Commonwealth commissioners who reviewed and granted the petition, reducing the rent to £100 'for this year, ending at May next and no more'.

It is difficult to avoid the conclusion that Corbet had been angling for Talbot's estate since they first crossed paths in February 1652. A month after Dean King's flight, and about the time of Talbot's imprisonment, Corbet revoked a licence issued by the revenue commissioners for 'the felling of timber trees about the castle and house of Malahide to be imployed for the repairing of a house in another town held in custodium', and ordered that 'timber be allowed out of some woods belonging to the Commonwealth for such necessary reparations and not any trees about any house that are for the beauty and ornament thereof'.[59] The imposition of a *cordon sanitaire* about Talbot's house suggests that it was already earmarked for Corbet. Subsequently, in 1653, he chose Malahide as a sanctuary against the plague in the knowledge that Talbot was an indicted outlaw and presently destined for Connacht. Possession being nine-tenths of the law, he was effectively staking a claim on the estate whenever Talbot should be transplanted and his support for a reduction in Talbot's rent guaranteed, when it finally devolved to him, that the estate was undervalued. He managed to drive the rent down to as low as £50 when he obtained a Commonwealth lease for the estate in late 1654 or early 1655 and had it renewed on the same terms in 1658 for a further twenty-one years.[60]

Corbet's use of Talbot's indictment as a means of gaining a foothold in Malahide is a signal reminder that with the surrender of the Irish royalists in May 1652, the Adventurers' act and Talbot's outlawry had finally become live issues. The first clause of the Commonwealth Act of Settlement of 1652, which prepared the ground for the transplantation of the outlaws, enacted that:

> All and every person and persons who at any time before the Tenth day of November, One thousand six hundred forty two … have contrived, advised, counselled, promoted or acted, the Rebellion, Murthers or Massacres done or committed in Ireland or have at any time before the said Tenth day of November, One thousand six hundred forty two, by bearing arms, or contributing Men, Arms, horse, Plate, Money, Victual, or other furniture or habiliaments of War [have] ayded, assisted, promoted, acted, prosecuted or abetted the said Rebellion, Murthers or Massacres, be excepted from Pardon of Life and Estate.[61]

Talbot had been outlawed in the first year of the rebellion and so under the terms of this article he was liable to the death penalty. It has been estimated that under this clause alone up to 80,000 people were liable to the death penalty but, in the event, though several hundred were executed between 1652 and 1654, the provision for capital punishment appears to have been quietly shelved.[62] He was also excepted from pardon of estate and so, unlike those coming under the fifth clause, the Confederate officers, who were to be granted a third of their estates 'in such places in Ireland, as the Parliament … shall think fitt to appoint for that purpose' for the benefit of their wives and children, Talbot should have had no expectation of receiving land in Connacht.[63] However, Cromwell's instructions to the Commonwealth commissioners in July 1653 to settle *all* forfeiting proprietors in Connacht and Clare before the 1 May 1654, confirmed by the act for satisfaction of the adventurers and soldiers passed on 26 September, meant that he must soon transplant there whatever his expectations.[64]

The extension of Talbot's custodium, granted in April 1654, for a year until May 1655, indicates that he had not transplanted by the appointed date in May 1654. Dispensations until May 1655 were freely granted, the petitioners no doubt pleading among other things, as the countess of Fingal had, that they had already sown crops.[65] The first transplantations had begun, however, although the administrative structure necessary to process the transplanted as they arrived in Connacht was not yet fully in place. A commission had been established at Loughrea in early 1654 to set out lands to the transplanted who were due to arrive by 1 May.[66] Transplanters arriving at Loughrea were assigned land 'proportional to their respective stocks and tillage in the places from whence they removed' according to the details contained on a certificate issued by the revenue commissioners in their local precinct.[67] This distribution began, however, before the entitlement of the arriving transplanters to land under the 1652 act had been determined. Hence, by December, when the court of qualifications (sitting in Athlone) was established to adjudicate on the transplanters' qualifications under the act and to determine the exact proportions of land which were to be finally set out to them by the Loughrea commissioners, many transplanters who had no entitlement to land by their qualifications were already settled in Connacht.[68] Equally ominous for those transplanting at a later date, the reservation of the counties of Sligo, Leitrim, Clare and the barony of Tirawley in county Mayo to meet the soldiers' arrears truncated the amount of land available for assignment to the transplanted and the land bank was further eroded when it was realised, in addition to the inward transplantation of forfeiting proprietors from Ulster, Leinster and Munster, that account had to be taken of the needs of forfeiting resident proprietors of Connacht and Clare.[69] By late 1654, then, the administrative process designed to effect the settlement of forfeiting proprietors had already been heavily compromised. In due course many Catholics excepted from pardon of life and estate would receive lands, in some cases very extensive acreages, while many who were entitled to land would discover that there was no land left to satisfy their claims.[70]

Talbot and his family, together with their livestock, victuals and any tenants willing to accompany them, made the long trek into Connacht between the winter of 1654–5 and early spring 1655, prompted by the sheriff of Dublin's proclamation that all who had as yet not transplanted should do so before the 10 January 1655 in order to have their claims determined.[71] Although not entitled to any consideration under the act of 1652, he may have gained consolation from an order of the Commonwealth commissioners which directed the Loughrea commission 'to set out a convenient habitation in Connaught for him'.[72] In the event that expectation was to prove unfounded. The Loughrea commissioners had made no provision for him by April 1655 and he was compelled to petition the Commonwealth to have their directive put into effect.[73] The Commonwealth commissioners readily confirmed their earlier directive, directing that he be 'accommodated with a convenient house and lands *de bene esse* according to his qualifications with consideration of the quality of what he is removed from'.[74] In appending the words '*according to his qualifications*' to their directive, however, the Commissioners effectively negated the apparently beneficial provisions it contained. Corbet, who had signed this order, knew Talbot's qualifications only too well, having employed them to usurp his estate. In the meantime Talbot and his family had spent the winter or early spring at Loughrea in some form of temporary accommodation waiting fruitlessly for the commissioners there to implement the directive and consuming whatever victuals they had carried with them into Connacht. With the sowing season now upon them and no land settlement in view, the possibility of starvation in the following year became a real and ugly prospect. In his petition to Charles II for restoration Talbot describes how ' he was like to starve, no provision in land being made for him as for others'.[75] To meet his more immediate needs while the outcome of his petition was being determined, Talbot successfully appealed for a safe-conduct pass from Connacht to Dublin in order 'to dispose of his corn and other goods'.[76] Clearly a crop had been harvested and stored at Malahide the previous autumn, only some of which the Talbots had been able to convey to Loughrea. There was a further pressing reason for returning to county Dublin. The fortunes of the Talbots had now plummeted to their lowest ebb and John Talbot felt impelled to make the traditional pilgrimage to St. Marnock's well at Portmarnock.

While Talbot's inoffensive existence at Malahide until 1652 can be interpreted as a pragmatic desire to secure the continuity of his lordship and inheritance in a fluctuating, dangerous world, his response to pivotal moments in his own life in the 1650s illustrates the deeper, enduring values he held. His loyalty to the crown, for example, manifested in unquestioned assistance to Dean King, clearly overrode the fear of retribution from the Commonwealth. His clandestine pilgrimage to Portmarnock in 1655, though a less significant affront, was no more calculated to incur the blessing of the puritan Commonwealth commissioners who abhorred and prohibited the 'practice of the Irish Papists in divers parts of this land yearly, and in a superstitious manner, [of] frequenting wells'.[77] Nevertheless, at the moment of greatest degradation, he emerged from Connacht to seek solace at the holy well in Portmarnock. His understandable bitterness towards Corbet's occupation of Malahide is recalled in the rhapsody in the acid conclusion to the story of his pilgrimage which recounts how he was 'more sorry he cod not goe to our ladys image by Corbets liveing in ye house'.[78] It is fitting, perhaps, in the light of Talbot's deep religious conviction and the consolation he found therein, that the only extant passage of direct speech attributable to him, 'You will never have anny blesing if you doe not observe her command' should be a commendation to his son Richard to uphold the Marian tradition of the family.[79]

Having made his pilgrimage and disposed of his corn and goods, Talbot returned to Connacht but continued to make little progress with the commission at Loughrea. He petitioned the Commonwealth commissioners yet again and a directive was issued 'that some lands to the value of £30 per annum should be assigned unto him as the Parliament's mercy and not as any compensation for his estate or anie part thereof.'[80] This was a critical adjudication. While the proceedings of the Athlone and Loughrea courts have perished, thereby casting a veil over whatever considerations were given to Talbot's case, it seems abundantly clear from the foregoing that he was to suffer the penalty of his qualifications, an exemption of pardon for estate and have but the benefit of a charity. In sharp contrast, other transplanters, such as Richard Barnewall and Lawrence Dowdall, who were actually named in the act of 1652 and transparently more 'guilty' than he, were destined to receive ample compensation in the form of large estates in Connacht.[81] The 'charity' extended to

Talbot appears, at first glance, to comprise a relatively substantial grant of land. In March 1656 he was decreed 1,000 acres.[82] According to Simington, Talbot's decree was to be effected in whole or in part in the baronies of Athlone, Roscommon and Ballintober in county Roscommon.[83] By June of that year, however, when a final settlement was made, the Loughrea commissioners were complaining that 'many baronies are totally exhausted'.[84] In the light of these constraints, John Talbot managed to secure only 333 acres in the townlands of Toberyoge, Gortinaglough, Corray and Cargin, parish of Kilmyan, in the barony of Athlone.[85] These townlands comprised the holdings of a native Irish sept, the O'Murrays, who were, in turn, transplanted to the neighbouring barony of Roscommon to accommodate the Talbots. The O'Murrays' decree of forty acres was to be realised in the parish of Elphin, but, as was the case with the Talbots, the actual amount of land they received fell very far short of their decree. Simington notes the O'Murrays of Kilmyan to be in receipt of just four acres at Elphin.[86]

The Talbots remained at Kilmyan until the close of the decade, the poll tax list of 1660 recording 'John Talbot Esq & his sonn gent' as tituladoes in the townland of Corry, in the same parish.[87] The history of the devolution of this holding subsequent to the Restoration remains something of a mystery. As a Connacht transplanter Talbot should have surrendered this land to the crown before receiving a re-grant of his former estate. Yet the books of survey and distribution for county Roscommon and the schedule of grants under the Restoration Act of Settlement show Richard Talbot of Malahide to have passed letters patent for the Kilmyan land.[88] Even more perplexing is the fact that the Talbot estate papers contain no reference to the Kilmyan holding. One possibility is that the Richard Talbot mentioned in the grant is John's brother, Richard, who, as we noted earlier, withdrew his claim before the court of claims for an annuity of £40 on the Talbot estates in counties Dublin and Louth. If Richard Talbot had truly been involved in the rebellion it may have been some advantage to John Talbot, in the sensitive circumstances of his attempts to retrieve his estate, to have this tincture of rebellion disappear into Connacht, Kilmyan being Richard's compensation for foregoing his annuity. A further possibility is that the Kilmyan land was actually granted to John's son, Richard. After John's death in 1671 Richard purchased some of the more valuable portions of forfeited Talbot land by selling off Castlering, one of the less profitable estates.[89] Kilmyan may also have been sold off to fund such transactions.

The collapse of the Commonwealth government in late 1659 lifted the cloud of misfortune that had dogged the Talbots for years. As the momentum for the restoration of the monarchy increased, the position of regicides such as Miles Corbet became precarious. Corbet was arrested coming from church but eluded his captors to join his fellow republican, Ludlow, on board the frigate *Oxford* in Dublin Bay on 31 December 1659 from whence they proceeded via Duncannon to London.[90] As a signatory to the death warrant of Charles I, he was, in due course, to be tried and executed. His flight, however, immediately opened up a precious window of opportunity to the Talbots to commence the struggle to regain their estates.

For the greater portion of the years between 1641 and 1659, and despite the momentous challenges presented by war and the establishment of the Commonwealth regime, John Talbot had managed to retain peaceful possession of the manor of Malahide. A critical factor in his survival during that period was his ability to exploit the recurring shortages of food and capital that persisted into the mid-1650s. Despite his connections with the defecting Catholic gentry of the Pale, he appears to have shunned active personal participation in the war but whether this was the cautious response of a man newly come to the lordship and anxious to preserve his estate or a reflection of traditional Talbot loyalty, or both, remains unclear. Neither, at any rate, prevented him from being outlawed, the grounds for which were questionable, but it did enable him to reach an accommodation with Ormonde who accepted that he was innocent of complicity in the war. Ormonde also recognised the stupidity of pursuing a scorched earth policy in Fingal, the city's granary, and it was on his urging that Malahide was spared the destruction visited on other Fingallian towns. As a supplier of victuals to the army Talbot consolidated his royalist credentials and, by remaining in situ, was able to enhance those credentials by assisting Dean King to escape to the Isle of Man. His assistance to Dean King earned him no credits with the Commonwealth but the risk he took in doing so and the punishment he suffered suggests that his loyalty was not simply an exigency of the moment. The ending of the war in 1652 and an improvement in the supply of foodstuffs in 1654 created the conditions in which the outlawries and the Adventurers' act became active. Given the all-embracing nature of the Commonwealth Act of Settlement, very few Catholic proprietors could have hoped to escape transplantation. John Talbot can have had no such expectations given his outlawry, his known royalist proclivities and Corbet's interest in acquiring his estate yet he clearly expected to be provided with some land in Connacht. The refusal of the Loughrea commissioners to settle him was a shattering blow, raising, in the short-term, the prospect of starvation. It was also an indication that the rules of the game had changed. With Ormonde, at least, he had shared a common loyalty and heritage, factors which could be employed to facilitate a mutual accommodation. Building a rapport with the Commonwealth was altogether a different matter. It may well be that Talbot's initial difficulty in acquiring land in Connacht is attributable to the fact that he was unwilling, or unable, to grease the palms of the Loughrea commissioners, at least some of whom were intent on enriching themselves.[91] His grant of land in Connacht appears to have been elicited by pestering the Commonwealth with petitions, a practice he would employ again after the Restoration, making a nuisance of himself until they yielded him a 'charity'.

Within the space of three years Talbot had found himself imprisoned, ejected from his house, transplanted with his family to Connacht and, finally, on the brink of starvation. In a world that was growing ever more disjointed and hostile, the pilgrimage he undertook to Portmarnock in 1655 can be interpreted as an attempt to retain a link with the old certainties of Talbot traditions and values and to find strength and hope in the guardian of those traditions and values, the Blessed Virgin.

# Surviving the Peace 1660–1671

The restoration of Charles II in 1660 should have been a blessing for Catholics like John Talbot who had maintained their royal account in credit at enormous personal expense during the darkest periods of the rebellion and interregnum. Given the king's known sympathies, Catholics generally looked forward to greater religious toleration and optimistically envisaged the dismantling of the Cromwellian settlement and the recovery of their land.[1] They certainly had as just a claim to favour as the 'old' Protestants (the settlers or descendants of settlers from the Tudor-Jacobean plantations), whose loyalty over the previous decades had shifted pragmatically from king to Commonwealth and finally back again, and a superior claim to the 'new' (i.e., Cromwellian) Protestants who had served the Commonwealth, for both were equally guilty of treason. In reality, however, the Stuart restoration was primarily a consequence of Protestant endeavours and, despite his sympathy for the plight of his Catholic subjects, Charles II proved unwilling to antagonise either the English parliament or the alliance of old and new Protestants in Ireland whose chief goal throughout the 1660s was to freeze the Cromwellian settlement.[2] The subsequent success of the Protestant interest in retaining the bulk of their land acquisitions derived, in the main, from the fact that the king's declaration of November 1660, which permitted the majority of soldiers and adventurers to keep their land, had, as Clarendon observed, 'wiped out the memory of the rebellion of the one, whilst the other is liable to all reproaches'.[3] In the final analysis, the claims of the competing groups were to prove incompatible and the success or failure of Catholics in retrieving their land would depend less on their apparent guilt or innocence during the rebellion than on their ability to draw on influential kinship and patronage ties in the Caroline court, access to capital, legal acumen, personal fortitude and even such random variables as geographical location and good fortune. All played a role, in varying degrees, in the eventual recovery of the greater part of the Talbot inheritance but the process of retrieval was to be slow and attended by many false dawns. Ranged against the Talbot interest were the interests of those who had been granted forfeited Talbot property in Garristown and Castlering during the interregnum and who would look to a similar set of resources to hold what they had gained. Heavily advantaged by their control of parliament and the indebtedness of a monarch whose restoration they had facilitated, the cards were stacked against a Talbot recovery. Having survived the war John Talbot now faced a no less arduous challenge, a struggle to survive the peace.

During the years of exile in Connacht the Talbots did not lose complete contact with their former estates. Despite repeated proclamations commanding the relatives of transplanters to transplant, John Talbot's brother Richard remained at Garristown, apparently throughout the Commonwealth period, and it was probably through him that notice of Corbet's flight was first received.[4] The initial reaction to the regicide's sudden departure can only have been jubilation for Malahide now lay open for repossession and the Talbots were spared the aggravation of ejecting incumbent planters. While Corbet's execution in 1662 meant that no further challenge to their entitlement to Malahide would emanate from that quarter, he did bequeath them an unexpected legacy. When the Talbots re-occupied Malahide they found themselves encumbered with his old Commonwealth rent of £50, for which they were now liable to the crown.[5] The repossession of Talbot properties in Garristown and Castlering was less easily achieved. At the Restoration the Garristown estate was occupied by a soldier and an adventurer, both of whom were in possession of Commonwealth leases. In 1658 Alexander Staples, of Lissan, county Tyrone, the son of an Ulster planter, obtained a ninety-nine year lease on Elizabeth Talbot's dower lands as a Cromwellian '49 officer.[6] Staples was heavily implicated in Colonel Thomas Blood's conspiracy in 1663 to seize Dublin castle and kidnap Ormonde, the lord lieutenant.[7] Although subsequently pardoned, he was nevertheless expelled from the house of commons in 1665 for complicity in the plot.[8] The remainder of the Talbot estate in that parish had been granted to an English Protestant widow, Susannah Bastwick, on the order of Oliver Cromwell. Bastwick was not strictly speaking an adventurer in that her grant originated not from any contribution to the adventurers' fund but from Cromwell's wish to recompense her for 'the Tyrannical illegal and cruel sentence given against her husband by his late Ma[jes]tie and his Councell'.[9] She did not take up residence in Ireland and subsequently disposed of her holding to Sir Audley Mervyn, speaker of the Irish house of commons, in the early 1660s. It is interesting to note that Mervyn's name was rarely publicly associated with his acquisition of the property until late in the 1660s, the assignment being generally denoted, as it was in the Act of Explanation, in terms such as 'such person or persons who purchased the same of and from Susannah Bastwick or her children'.[10] Thus, Mervyn was able to attack any attempts to undo the Cromwellian settlement without appearing to have a personal interest. In many ways Mervyn was the representative *par excellence* of the 'old' Protestant settlers whose treasonable activities the king proved so willing to overlook. In the view of one commentator he was a chameleon who 'could comply with the times, and be a royalist, or a parliamentarian, even a covenanter, as the pressure of the occasion required'.[11] Such dexterity, allied with his prominence in parliament, made him a formidable opponent, well equipped politically to stymie Talbot's attempts to retrieve Garristown.

As the bulk of county Louth had not been assigned away by the time of the Commonwealth collapse, Talbot property at Castlering had been held in custodium by the Exchequer and continued as such into the early years of the Restoration.[12] Talbot petitioned successfully for a custodium of the premises but when it came up for renewal in 1663, acting apparently on advice which suggested that 'it may be of some prejudice to ... take the premises in his owne name', he applied to have the terms of the custodium altered to read 'for the use of and in trust for the said John Talbot'.[13] While Talbot's request was being processed through the court of exchequer, however, he was gazumped and the custodium was granted to John Clotworthy, first viscount Massarene.[14] Clotworthy had claims on the crown that far exceeded Talbot's. He had assented to the king's request to yield his adventure in Antrim to Daniel O' Neill, the king's groom of the bedchamber, in return for reprisals in counties Kildare and Louth.[15] The king's obligation to him for facilitating O'Neill clearly placed Clotworthy in a powerful bargaining position. By this stage there was very little custodium land available in county Louth and Castlering became the means by which his reprisals were to be satisfied in that county. Like Staples, both Clotworthy and Mervyn appear to have been complicit in Blood's conspiracy. Writing to Clarendon in January, 1664, Sir Alan Broderick, a judge in the court of claims, observed 'nor are there yet proofs against Massarene and the speaker [Audley Mervyn] though his grace knows, by dubitable circumstances they were both privy to the conspiracy'.[16] The willingness of this triumvirate to consider illicit as well as licit means to secure their grants is an indication of the lengths they would go to frustrate Talbot's restoration. Although he cannot have known it then, the loss of the custodium on Castlering in May 1663 effectively ended John Talbot's personal interest in the property. Had he retained an interest there until the 22 August he would have been able to effect complete restoration. Under Clause CLVII of the Act of Explanation, letterees, those in possession of king's letters, were to be fully restored, provided they were in occupation on 22 August 1663 of property that they, or their ancestors, had seisin of on 22 October 1641. The Talbot family interest was not completely ended, however. When John Skeffington, Clotworthy's heir, succeeded in having letters patent passed confirming the grant of Castlering, a savings clause was appended to the patent which limited his tenure to the life of John Talbot, at which time the estate would devolve to Talbot's son Richard.[17]

At the Restoration all forfeited land reverted to the Crown and so in order to acquire a secure title to his estate Talbot's first recourse in 1660 was to submit a petition to the king. The substance of Talbot's claim, his unswerving loyalty, his quiet occupation of Malahide and the penalties he endured as a consequence of his assistance to Dean King were readily accepted and supported by Sir Maurice Eustace and by Ormonde and a letter confirming Talbot in his estate as it existed prior to the rebellion was issued in November 1660.[18]

Significantly, it directed that adventurers or soldiers occupying part of his estate should be 'forthwith reprised' with lands elsewhere. This directive complied with the king's 'Gracious Declaration' of the same month, the construction of which was heavily influenced by both Clotworthy and Mervyn. It confirmed the adventurers and soldiers in their holdings and ordered immediate reprisals to those who might be dislodged in order to accommodate the restoration of Catholics who could prove their innocence before the commissioners appointed to execute the declaration.[19] The ability of Catholics to prove their innocence was severely circumscribed by a complex series of instructions which were issued in February 1661 to give effect to the declaration. Catholics were not to be restored who had 'enjoyed their estates … in the rebels quarters [unless] expelled from [English] quarters and driven into quarters of the rebels', a clause which certainly encompassed John Talbot.[20] Even had Talbot applied to the commission it is unlikely that he would have succeeded. Mervyn had been appointed as one of the thirty commissioners and hence would have been required to adjudicate on Talbot's claim to land in Garristown which he himself had acquired through the purchase of Bastwick's debenture. To judge by the comments of another commissioner, Francis, Lord Aungier, impartiality was not one of Mervyn's better qualities. Writing to Ormonde in April 1661, he declared that 'self interest and partiality, not justice, is the rule for judging there and … Sir Audley Mervyn who always gives the rule in this court is the most partial judge on earth'.[21] However, as the declaration was construed in Ireland to have no statutory authority, no serious attempt was made to execute its provisions. In the period between its publication and the statutory enactment of its provisions in the Act of Settlement in July 1662, Mervyn and Staples rebuffed an attempt by Talbot to dislodge them on the strength of the king's letter. Details regarding this attempt and the grounds on which it was resisted can be inferred from the internal evidence contained in a second letter which Talbot was compelled to obtain from the king in June 1661.[22] Mervyn and Staples appear to have withstood Talbot's challenge by referring to the declaration's confirmation of the holdings of soldiers and adventurers and to the fact that no reprisals had been offered. Critically, they also invoked Talbot's indictment and transplantation and pointed out that they were paying crown rent on the property. On this basis it seems unlikely that Talbot would have been able to persuade the county sheriff that he had sufficient cause to evict them. Talbot petitioned the king again and the king's response opened up a legal avenue which he proceeded to employ throughout the decade to oust the settlers. Essentially, Talbot realised that if he succeeded in having their rents put out of charge they would not then be in a position to claim that they were legally in occupation and the king's letter of restoration could be executed.

Responding to Talbot's petition, the king noted that Talbot could not enjoy the benefits of the first letter 'by reason of some outlawry appearing of record

against him' and ordered that he be 'forthwith possessed and confirmed in the
quiet and peaceable possession of the sayd former estates … notwithstanding
any indictment or outlawry of record against him, and notwithstanding his
said acceptance of a charity or interest in the province of Connaught'.[23]
Furthermore, the court of Exchequer was directed to 'forbeare writeing for
any such rents soo putt in charge on the said lands or any part thereof since
the said month of October 1648 for it is our express will and pleasure the
same to be suspended until our letters patent containing a pardon and restitution to the said John Talbot as aforesaid or untill such indictment and outlawry be taken away by an Act of Oblivion and Indemnity'. A more fulsome
letter of restoration could hardly have been envisaged by Talbot. He was now
in a position to proceed in the court of exchequer to have the crown rents put
out of charge and achieve full seisin of the property. While in the long term
the king's letters would prove of some value, in an immediate practical sense
they were worthless. Their ineffectuality can really only be understood in the
terms of the complete bureaucratic muddle that existed in Whitehall. Talbot
was 'restored' by king's letter in November 1660 yet in January 1661 Malahide
was also granted to Sir James Shaen *de bene esse* in anticipation of the passing
of letters patent.[24] In February it was included in a schedule of lands desig-
nated for the earl of Mountrath and not to be disposed of 'till he had been
fully satisfied'.[25] On 17 June Talbot's restoration was ordered 'forthwith' yet a
year later Shaen was confirmed in his concession.[26] Finally, in December
1662, the king was 'anxious to restore Talbot'.[27] The Act of Settlement passed
in July 1662 added little clarity to the situation. Well might the king acknowledge that 'the laying of the foundations is not now before us, when we
might design the model of the structure answerable to our own thoughts', for
Talbot, a nominee in the act, was yet again to be 'forthwith restored … with
the same advantages, benefits and assurances to all intents and purposes as the
lord visc. Nettervil, and the lord visc. Galmoy', effectively without being put
to further proof of innocence.[28] In the same act, however, the widow Bastwick
was confirmed in her holding at Garristown and the lands held by regicides
during the Commonwealth, as Malahide was, were vested in the king's brother,
the duke of York.[29] The Talbot estate in county Dublin was thus granted and
re-granted no less than eight times in the space of twenty months. The issuing
of so many contradictory letters can only have caused immeasurable confusion
to officials in the Exchequer on whom the task of executing the various directives would have fallen. In the circumstances, doing nothing appeared to be
the safest option.

Armed with his letters, Talbot appeared in the court of exchequer in trinity
term, 1661, seeking to have the rents on Malahide and Garristown put out of
charge but only succeeded in having them suspended until Michaelmas, the
court sitting which commenced in September.[30] In August, however, Staples
succeeded in passing letters patent which copperfastened his hold on Talbot

land in Garristown.[31] Frustrated at his failure to secure a custodium on Castlering in 1663, Talbot appeared again in the court of exchequer during Michaelmas 1664 pleading the privilege of his king's letter to have Clotworthy's rent put out of charge and to be 'confirmed in the quiet possession of all and singular his former estate' only to be adjudged a similarly brief suspension.[32] The suspension, as opposed to the putting out of charge, of the rents appears to suggest an element of temporising on the part of the judge. A permanent order of respit properly executed by the sheriff should have resulted in re-possession but as Talbot did not recover seisin of Garristown or Castlering the suspensions appear to have constituted no more than temporary injunctions, without effect on the sitting tenants. Had Talbot succeeded in effecting a per-manent writ of respit neither Clotworthy, Staples nor Mervyn could have claimed to be in possession by payment of rent and his restoration would have been facilitated. On both occasions such an eventuality was blocked by John Bysse, recorder of Dublin during the interregnum and now a judge in the court of exchequer, whose granting of brief suspensions effectively consigned the cases to limbo. Exasperated by his inability to have the king's letters en-forced and by his lack of progress in the exchequer court, Talbot forcibly dis-possessed Mervyn in 1662 and re-occupied Garristown. The speaker responded by bringing the full weight of parliament against him, eliciting a directive from his parliamentary colleagues to the sheriff of county Dublin which ordered him to 'restore and quiet unto the said Sir Audley Mervyn or his assigns, the possession of the towns and lands [of Garristown] ... and to take care that he be no further disquieted therein'.[33]

Although Talbot persisted in pursuing his claims through the exchequer throughout the decade, the financial burdens imposed by repeated petitioning and litigation clearly placed enormous strains on his resources. Initially, at least, it proved difficult to extract capital from Malahide. In 1660 'the lands of Malahide being for the most part waste and yielding no profit', the tithes were demised to Ralph Wallis for £12, just barely above the sum of £11.6s.8d for which they had been leased to Robert Jans over one hundred years earlier.[34] Additionally, upon re-occupying Malahide, Talbot found himself encumbered with Corbet's old Commonwealth rent. By 1661 he was also paying a 'sub-sidy', the poll tax, a custodium rent on Castlering and was later liable for the hearth tax.[35] The estrangement of Garristown and Clotworthy's success in ac-quiring Castlering meant that he could not draw financially on those estates and so from 1663 he was totally reliant on Malahide to fund his legal challenges. The capacity of the Malahide estate to generate the ready cash required to pay scriveners, court and attorney fees or any of the petty bribes which were a pre-requisite to the prosecution of his claims had already been eroded by the usurpation of the entitlement to the customs of the port. The customs had been assigned during the Commonwealth period to Ralph Hughes and crown waiters were appointed there from 1660.[36] Shorn of this entitlement, Talbot was compelled, at least once, in 1662, to resort to the merchant Christian Borr to obtain what can only have been a diminutive sum of money given that the repayment was a mere £45.[37] In time, as the prospect of recovering the estate through litigation diminished, new financial burdens would be incurred in the pursuit of that goal that would disable the Talbots economically into the following century.

The Act of Settlement of 1662 formally vested in the crown all land confiscated as a consequence of the 1641 rebellion with the exception of land held on 22 October 1641 by Catholics or Protestants who could prove in a court of claims to be established by the act that they were innocent of any rebellious activity. Claimants awarded a decree of innocence in this court were to be restored to land to which they could claim a valid title and since the decree merely confirmed their innocence they were not required to pass new letters patent. Although John Talbot was a nominee in the act and to be restored forthwith without being put to further proof of innocence, his reversals in connection with Garristown and Castlering indicate that such favour could not be taken at face value. The court of claims, however, offered him an opportunity to cast off the shadow of outlawry which had dogged him since 1642 and which had constituted a persistent obstacle to the recovery of his estate. Equally important, it enabled his sister Jane and son Richard to establish their inheritance rights. The court opened on 13 January 1663 having received in advance a schedule of the lands claimed by the applicant together with a statement of the grounds on which the decree was sought. As the court had decided to hear the claims of proprietors from Dublin city and county first, claimants from that area were particularly favoured in terms of the number of decrees granted. Talbot's case came before the court on 2 April 1663, where he elected to state his claim not on his innocence of participation in the rebellion but on his proviso in the Act of Settlement and the king's letter.[38] As it transpired, this was of little consequence. In determining the order in which claims would be heard the court followed the precedence established in the Act of Settlement whereby those seeking a decree of innocence who had not accepted land as transplanters were to be heard first. Thus, Talbot's claim was immediately postponed and by the time the court closed in August of that year the claims of transplanters had not yet been heard.[39] In theory, then, when the implications of the vesting of the estates of the regicides in James, duke of York, are taken into account, Talbot's postponement created the frightening prospect of the family being left landless. Fortunately, Talbot had taken the precaution of submitting a joint claim with his son and this was heard. Richard's claim was based on his grandfather's will in which the estate was entailed for life.[40] As the law held that the heir inherited through the original grantor, in this case Richard the grandfather who had died prior to the rebellion, the postponement of John Talbot's case had no bearing on young Richard's claim. Richard was decreed innocent and his entitlement in remainder after John's death was upheld.[41] Jane Talbot's claim was heard on 20 August, the day before the court shut down permanently.[42] Her claim was also based on the will of the elder Richard in which he bequeathed her an annual sum of £40 out of the manors of Malahide, Garristown and Castlering together with a payment of £100 upon her marriage or the age of seventeen years whichever should fall first. She claimed a further £800 as her portion were she to marry with the consent of the trustees of the will. She, too, was decreed innocent and therefore entitled to receive the benefit of the bequest.

The operation of the court of claims set up under the Act of Settlement inflamed emotions on all sides. Protestants renounced it for having restored so many Catholics whereas Catholics were dissatisfied that it had closed before many claimants had been given an opportunity to press their claims. As early as February 1663 Mervyn delivered twenty proposals in the house of commons to restrict the powers of the commissioners in the court of claims and which suggested that the widest possible construction be put on the term 'innocence'.[43] It is likely that at least some of Mervyn's strident opposition owed something to the fear that he was about to be ousted from Garristown. Equally, the participation of Staples in Blood's plot in May 1663, a month after Talbot's case had come before the court of claims, may be traced from the court's earlier adjudication that young Richard Talbot was innocent and to be restored in remainder after his father's death. As John Talbot was now in his mid-fifties, Staples may have envisaged the possibility of a premature termination of his ninety-nine year lease.

The complications raised by the adjudications of the court of claims reflected what had been apparent even before the passing of the Act of Settlement, that a further explanatory act would be required to resolve the innumerable deficiencies in the earlier legislation. A process of intensive lobbying ensued in London where the various factions attempted to impose their own particular spin on the proposed act. While there is no evidence to suggest that John Talbot had enlisted the aid of lobbyists to secure the king's letters or to ensure his nomination in the Act of Settlement, his setback in the court of claims appears to have encouraged him to draw down heavily on family connections in the royal court in pursuit of a more favourable settlement. In this respect he was unusually advantaged. His cousin, Richard Talbot of Carton, later earl of Tyrconnell, and his wife's uncle, Sir Nicholas Plunkett, were the principal agents for Catholics in London.[44] Richard Talbot had served in the exiled Stuart court and was a particular favourite of the duke of York. It was probably influence exerted through this connection that persuaded the duke to forego his entitlement to Corbet's former holding for no serious attempt was ever made to prosecute the regicide clause in the Act of Settlement against the Malahide estate. Plunkett was an eminent lawyer and may have devised the tactic of loosening Mervyn's grip on Garristown by focusing on the circumstances which attended the original grant to Bastwick.

While the Act of Explanation was being prepared at Worcester House in April 1665, John Talbot submitted a petition highlighting Cromwell's insult to Charles I which accompanied the Bastwick grant.[45] The committee acknowledged, were Talbot's allegations true, that he should be immediately restored to that part of the estate which had been demised to Bastwick. However, Lord Kingston, like Mervyn an acquirer of adventurers' debentures, was a member of the committee and it may have been through his influence that the codicil ordering prior reprisals to Bastwick or her purchasers was retained. Plunkett mounted a further challenge the following month, again emphasising Cromwell's denigration of the late king but focusing more trenchantly on the contradiction between the terms of Bastwick's proviso and those of the nominees in the Act of Settlement and the draft Act of Explanation:

> that such a proviso [Bastwick's] so grounded should adventure to seek y[ou]r Ma[jes]ties approbation in this and the former Act of Settlement must certainly be a surprize for want of due information otherwise soe scandalous an order of the usurpers could not obtaine from y[ou]r Ma[jes]tie an approbation in Parl[liame]nt or elsewhere but ought to be rejected rather that the confirming thereof tends to the prejudice of some of the 56 persons named in y[ou]r Ma[jes]ties declaration, whom you direct to be restored to their former estates without further proofe, and of some of the former proprietors, who suffered eminently by their endeavours to serve y[ou]r Ma[jes]tie.[46]

Despite Plunkett's lobby, the Bastwick grant was not undermined and when the Act of Explanation was passed later in 1665 Talbot's individual proviso ordered his restoration to all Talbot lands in county Dublin provided that 'such person or persons who purchased the same of and from Susannah Bastwick or her children or their assigns, being first satisfied out of the forfeited lands undisposed by this act … and after such restitution … the said John Talbot shall hold and enjoy, to him and his heirs, all and singular the lands, tenements and hereditaments so restored but subject to quit-rents'.[47]

A second court of claims was established to process in detail the various provisos in the act. It was procedurally similar to the earlier court except that in cases such as Talbot's, where the estate in question had been forfeited, a decree was issued in the form of a certificate containing the details and grounds of the court's adjudication. This certificate was then used to obtain a fiant from the lord lieutenant to pass letters patent. Since the estate being conveyed was a re-grant of a forfeited estate, successful claimants were liable for quit-rents which, as we have seen, were imposed on Talbot by the Act of Explanation. Talbot's claim was exhibited in February 1666 and his decree granted in July of that year. The details of the decree are to be found in a certificate which issued in June 1667.[48] It repeats verbatim the provision for reprisals for Bastwick's assigns but at this late stage, with the agents of the duke of York

trawling the counties Dublin and Louth in search of compensatory reprisals
for land York had been deprived of by decrees of the courts of claims, it was
unlikely that sufficient reprisals could be found to satisfy Mervyn. Hence,
while Talbot's certificate notes his entitlement to a life interest to two-thirds
of Garristown and Malahide, in the end he was able to execute this provision
on Malahide only. Both Mervyn's decree, enrolled in July 1668 and comprising a total of 1,282 acres in Garristown, and that of Staples (enrolled September
1666) for 621 acres, contained savings clauses to protect the interests of Richard
and Jane Talbot who had been declared innocent by the first court of claims
but these were to fall due only after John Talbot's death.

The value of the savings clauses appended to decrees of the courts of claims
has been questioned. Lawrence Arnold maintained that after 1669 the land
records are devoid of reference to them and he found few indications to suggest that they resulted in any significant shift in land ownership.[49] Forfeited
Talbot properties in Garristown and Castlering were subject to such clauses
and while direct primary evidence is not always available to clarify how the
Talbots attempted to enforce them, there are sufficient grounds to indicate
that they did facilitate the recovery of some of that property. An inquisition
post-mortem conducted on Mervyn's death reveals that he was seised of 1,280
acres in Garristown when he died in 1675, the exact amount of land which
had been decreed to him in 1668.[50] Nevertheless, by the 1690s Richard Talbot
was executing leases and mortgages on Baldwinstown, Tobergregan and
Newtown in Garristown, three of the townlands that had been decreed to
Mervyn. A chancery inquisition of 1708 which provides details of these transactions also contains the deposition of Oliver Todderick, a Newtown farmer,
who maintained that he had been Talbot's tenant for twenty-six years, indi-
cating that at least some of the land had been recovered as early as 1682.[51] The
extent of that recovery can be ascertained from a 1788 rent roll of the Talbot
holdings in Garristown which summarises Talbot holdings in that parish at
1,264 acres, almost equivalent to the pre-1641 holding of 1,330 acres to which
Talbot had sought to be restored in the court of claims.[52]

Although it is unclear how this land was recovered, proceedings in relation
to Staples' holding and the manner in which Castlering was retrieved suggest
one possibility. Since the king's letters, legislative provisos and suits in the court
of exchequer had only partially advanced the recovery of their estate, the
Talbots clearly had no reason to place any great trust in the enforceability of
savings clauses. Rather than wait for them to fall due, John and Richard Talbot
opened negotiations with Staples shortly after his decree was issued to purchase 519 acres, the greater part of his ninety-nine year crown lease and the
former dower lands of Elizabeth Talbot. Agreement was reached in December
1666 and an indenture tripartite was perfected between the Talbots, Staples
and John Graydon and Ralph Wallis (farmer of the tithes of Malahide) by
which Staples conveyed the land in return for 'the sume of four hundred and

fifty pounds one hundred and fifty pounds whereof hath been already paid
and the other three hundred pounds is hereby secured and paid'.[53] Graydon
and Wallis undertook to pay the remaining £300 by six half-yearly payments
in return for the use of the land until the Talbots re-imbursed them. An ac-
knowledgement appended to the indenture by Staples in May 1670 confirms
that the full sum had been paid so that once the Talbots re-paid Graydon and
Wallis the land was theirs. While Staples holding was recovered by purchase,
Castlering appears to have been recovered through the courts. When John
Talbot died in 1671 the savings clause in Clotworthy's decree became active
and Richard Talbot commenced an action for its recovery.[54] Talbot may have
received some assistance in prosecuting his case from John Keating, chief justice of the common pleas, for by an indenture dated 24 November 1682,
Keating purchased the manor of Castlering from Talbot for the sum of £2,725
sterling.[55] The significance of the date of this indenture should not be overlooked. It coincides with the earliest reference to Talbot leases on lands previ-
ously held by Mervyn, the implication being that Richard Talbot used the
money generated by the sale of Castlering to recover the bulk of outstanding Talbot property in Garristown.

John Talbot never lived to witness the *denouement* in relation to Castlering
and Garristown, nor indeed could he have, for their recovery was only made
possible by his death. During the last two years of his life he maintained the
struggle to retrieve the residue of his estate. In January 1669 he submitted yet
another petition and in November 1670 he endorsed Richard Talbot of Carton
as agent of the Irish Catholics in London, mandating him to prosecute 'one
or more peticons to his sacred Ma[jes]tie and his Parliament in England and
declaring ye complaints and grievances of his said subjects and therein to
seeke redresse'.[56] Talbot's signature at the foot of this commission reflects perhaps the weariness of a decade of frustration and the sense that individual
grievances might only be properly addressed by concerted, collective action.
In that respect, the marriage in 1670 of his son Richard to Frances Talbot,
daughter of Sir Robert Talbot of Carton, had a more than usual significance,
representing as it did the re-emergence of the Talbot tradition of forging links
within Old English Catholic society and an affirmation of the continuity of
Old English culture and values within the Pale.[57]

The accepted version of the history of the Talbots of Malahide in the seventeenth century is a simple one. They forfeited their lands in 1641 and were
subsequently restored because they had influence in the royal court.[58] The evidence advanced here suggests that this plot requires considerable amendment.
In the first instance, for a family of such reputed influence, the returns from
that source were far from overwhelming. The prominence of the Talbots of
Shrewsbury in the Caroline court appears to have contributed nothing to the
advancement of Talbot's restoration and while it is clear that John Talbot had
a line into Whitehall through Nicholas Plunkett and Richard Talbot of Carton,

and that both appear to have batted for him on occasions, it is unlikely that such connections enabled him to wield a disproportionate influence in the pursuit of his claims. By 1670 Malahide was the only Talbot property securely in his possession, facilitated partly through the good fortune accruing from Corbet's regicide, and the toehold in Garristown had been acquired through purchase. The inheritance rights of Richard and Jane Talbot had been secured in the court of claims yet theirs, together with the bulk of the estate, was an uncertain future under questionable savings clauses. Conjecturally, Talbot's various letters and provisos may have been the fruits of lobbying by Plunkett and Richard Talbot of Carton but the support of the Ormonde and Sir Maurice Eustace for Talbot's restoration suggests that they, too, were more than well disposed to recognise Talbot's loyalty and service. In direct opposition to Talbot's connections in court, and effectively negating them, was the influential Sir Audley Mervyn. His claims on Garristown were a significant counterbalancing impediment to Talbot's restoration throughout the 1660s. Successfully concealing his interest in that property, he was able to oppose the general restoration of Catholics in parliament as though he was a disinterested party in the proceedings. The incorporation of Bastwick's proviso in the acts of Settlement and Explanation, despite the odious reference to the king's father associated with that grant, demonstrates that he had a far stronger influence over the outcome of the settlement than John Talbot. His direct line was probably through Lord Kingston, a member of the committee at Worcester House which was drafting the Act of Explanation and the recipient of a grant of the forfeited estate of the Catholic Robert Preston at Balmadun which is situated immediately south of Mervyn's holdings in Garristown.[59] Coincidentally, John Bysse, the exchequer judge who thwarted Talbot's attempts to have the rents on Garristown and Castlering definitively put out of charge, held the bulk of his estate in a number of townlands due east of Garristown.[60] Thus, Talbot's attempts to recover Garristown floundered against competition which was more powerfully connected and which was probably intent on establishing a thoroughly Protestant proprietorship in that part of north-west county Dublin. In the final analysis, John Talbot's recovery, partial though it was, was effected by a range of factors. Some of these factors, legal trusts, influence in the royal court and loyalty to the crown, for example, were an intrinsic feature of the Talbot inheritance. Others evolved as circumstances dictated. The failure to procure a full restoration on the strength of the king's letters and the disappointments in the court of Exchequer and the courts of claims made him realise that the only way to break the stalemate in Garristown was by making it financially worthwhile for Staples to vacate the land.

# Conclusion

This study has attempted to identify the strategies which enabled the Talbots of Malahide to survive the upheavals created by the 1641 rebellion and to discover the extent to which the cultural and economic resources of that family helped John Talbot to buck the trend of a social revolution which decimated Catholic landownership in the seventeenth century. At his death in 1671, Talbot had retrieved only 1,124 acres (or one-third of his 1640 estate), the customs of the port of Malahide had been sequestered to crown use and the remainder of his property, a total of 2,716 acres, at Garristown and Castlering, remained in the hands of Cromwellian settlers. However, he had managed to repossess the most profitable land at Malahide and, together with the acquisition of Staples' holding at Garristown, had laid the foundations for subsequent Talbot attempts to regain the outstanding properties.

A feature of this study has been the extent to which John Talbot's survival and restoration was a consequence not of any single factor or influence but the product of a broad range of attitudes, values and traditions which were an integral part of the Talbot identity long before he acceded to the lordship and which related primarily to land, politics and religion. The initial challenge to John Talbot during the war and interregnum was to retain possession of the land and it was his ability to exploit the double advantage of the fertility of the soil of Malahide and its maritime location to survive that period. The contribution of Malahide's fishery to the city markets preserved that town from the destruction visited on other Fingallian towns and, despite his indictment, John Talbot was able to extend his own and the town's immunity right into the 1650s by living inoffensively, by victualling Ormonde's army and by supplying the city during food shortages. The manor, however, was as much a social as a geographical concept and by staying put and adapting to wartime conditions he also succeeded in holding the social fabric of the manor intact. That much is clear from the fealty shown by his fishermen in carrying him to Lambay ahead of Ormonde's army in 1642 and again, ten years later, when they transported Dean King to the Isle of Man and in their refusal to give evidence before Corbet. The restoration of Malahide was facilitated by the good fortune accruing from Corbet's regicide but this is only partially true. While Corbet's occupation of Malahide was a calculated move to acquire one of the most profitable estates in the county, it was also a tribute to the way in which Talbot had administered the manor during the war years. In this regard it is interesting to note that during the thirty-one years of Talbot's lordship, he retained possession of Malahide for all but the five years of his exile in Connacht. Given the economic cost of the protracted litigation and petitioning he undertook in the 1660s and the fact that eventually he had to purchase Staples' interest in Garristown, the ability to draw on the resources of Malahide, the most profitable part of his inheritance, was a considerable advantage.

The land question was intimately related to politics in that all land titles derived from the crown and were contingent upon the manifestation of continued loyalty. Although the evidence suggests that John Talbot side-stepped involvement in the rebellion, he was, nevertheless, outlawed and the Adventurers' act and the Cromwellian Act of Settlement ensured that he paid for that indictment with the sequestration of his property. Yet his demeanour throughout the war, and even during the Commonwealth period, suggests that his loyalty was no less unstinting than that displayed by his ancestor, Sir John Talbot, during the Nine Years War. Ormonde and Eustace appear to have had no doubts about his loyalty and his contribution to the army and the assistance he rendered to Dean King elicited the king's letters, which, though they did not succeed in restoring him, nevertheless became part of the arsenal he employed in pursuit of that goal.

While, overtly, John Talbot's devout Catholicism played but a tangential role in his struggle for restoration, its importance at a personal level in providing him with the psychological strength to persist during the darker moments in Connacht should not be overlooked. At a wider level, Catholicism, co-operation in conveyances to use and marriage patterns, themselves intrinsically bound up with the issues of land and politics, created an Old English nexus of mutual interest which John Talbot was able to exploit. Richard Talbot's conveyance to use, perfected in 1619 and modified by his will in 1640, became the basis on which the entitlements of young Richard Talbot and Jane Talbot were upheld in the court of claims and led ultimately to the retrieval of Castlering. Although it is not clear whether he took advantage of his connection through marriage with the lawyer and Catholic agent Nicholas Plunkett or of the influence of his cousin Richard Talbot of Carton with the duke of York in the early years of the Restoration, John Talbot certainly drew on Plunkett's legal acumen in 1665 to attack Bastwick's proviso in the Act of Explanation and it seems unlikely that Richard Talbot of Carton would have failed to use his influence to prompt the duke of York to forego his entitlement to Malahide under the regicide clause.

John Talbot, himself, appears to have had a considerable knowledge of the law, or had access to such knowledge, and the 1660s provided him with plenty of opportunities to employ it, most notably in his efforts to have the rents on Garristown and Castlering put out of charge. Had his attempts succeeded, he would have been able to regain seisin of those properties. That he was unable to do so was a consequence of the strength of opposition provided by Staples, Clotworthy and, particularly, Sir Audley Mervyn. The king's indebtedness to

Clotworthy for facilitating Daniel O'Neill terminated John Talbot's life interest in Castlering and Mervyn's prominence in the house of commons, his outspoken opposition to any softening of the Cromwellian settlement, his legal expertise and his connections with Lord Kingston, ensured that there would be no budging at Garristown throughout the 1660s. At the end of the day, the Restoration had been facilitated by Protestant interests and the king's obligation to a loyal Catholic subject was always going to be trumped, as Talbot's proviso in the Act of Explanation was, by that fact. His decision to purchase Staples' holding in the mid-1660s suggests a cold recognition of that reality as much as it represented a change in strategy. His endorsement of Richard Talbot as Catholic agent in 1670 was an elaboration of that tactical adjustment. Having exhausted all legal avenues, John Talbot had come to realise that only a complete dismantling of the land settlement would ensure a full restoration and that that might only be achieved through collective action.

The Talbot recovery, then, was no accident of history. The genesis of that recovery lay in John Talbot's inheritance and comprised a particular orientation to land and inheritance, loyalty to the crown, marriage alliances, legal acumen, economic resources and religious belief. It was an inheritance that he was able to capitalise on and exploit and which proved resilient in the face of the most dramatic social revolution in Irish history since the arrival of the Normans.

# Appendices

*Leading Fingallian proprietors ranked by estate size*

| Proprietor | Barony | Religion | Acreage | Valuation | £ per acre |
|---|---|---|---|---|---|
| Barnewall, Nich. | N, B, C | Catholic | 4017.5 | 1308.5 | 0.325 |
| Howth, Thos. Lord | N, B, C | Protestant | 3609 | 1217.5 | 0.337 |
| Dublin, Archbishop | N | Protestant | 2189.5 | 798.5 | 0.364 |
| Hollywood, Nich. | N, B, C | Catholic | 1547 | 427 | 0.276 |
| Bath, Jas. Drum | C | Catholic | 1280 | 830 | 0.648 |
| Barry, Sr Jas. | B, C | Protestant | 1160 | 557 | 0.48 |
| Netterfield, Luke | N, B | Catholic | 1117 | 275.75 | 0.246 |
| Preston, Robt. | B | Catholic | 1060 | 253 | 0.238 |
| Thomond, Lord | B | Protestant | 1040 | 240 | 0.23 |
| Plunkett, Jas. | N, C | Catholic | 1003 | 486 | 0.484 |
| Talbot, Eliz. | B | Catholic | 914 | 207.75 | 0.227 |
| Bamewall, Jas. | N, C | Protestant | 900 | 448 | 0.497 |
| Travers, Wm. | N, B | Catholic | 855 | 183 | 0.214 |
| Agar, John | C | Protestant | 800 | 600 | 0.75 |
| Dublin, City of | C | Protestant | 786 | 470 | 0.597 |
| Fagan, Chris. | B, C | Catholic | 766 | 376 | 0.49 |
| Omnond, Lord | B | Protestant | 60 | 132 | 0.173 |
| Finglas, John Wpltn | B | Catholic | 731 | 225 | 0.307 |
| Bolton, Sr Edwd. | N, B, C | Protestant | 700 | 279.5 | 0.399 |
| Blakeney, Geo. | N, B, C | Catholic | 698 | 217.75 | 0.311 |
| Bysse, John | N, B, C | Protestant | 692 | 168 | 0.242 |
| Gomnanstown, Ld | NB | Catholic | 681 | 146 | 0.214 |
| Cruse, Chr. | B | Catholic | 672 | 146.4 | 0.217 |
| Christchurch | N, B, C | Protestant | 618 | 365 | 0.59 |
| Finglas, Eliz. | B | Catholic | 617 | 140 | 0.226 |
| Bamewall, Matt. | B | Catholic | 587 | 152.15 | 0.259 |
| King, Geo. | C | Catholic | 560 | 28 | 0 0.5 |
| Dungan, Edwd. | B | Catholic | 510 | 140 | 0.274 |
| Talbot, John Mal | N, C | Catholic | 501.5 | 300.75 | 0.599 |

**C** = Coolock, **B** = Balrothery, **N** = Nethercross, **Valuation** = Aggregated
annual rental value, **£ per acre** = Rental value per acre

## APPENDIX 2

*Leading Fingallian proprietors ranked by annual rental value*

| Proprietor | Barony | Religion | Acreage | Valuation | £ per acre |
|---|---|---|---|---|---|
| Barnewall, Nich. | N, B, C | Catholic | 4017.5 | 1308.5 | 0.325 |
| Howth, Thos. Lord | N, B, C | Protestant | 3609 | 1217.5 | 0.337 |
| Bath, Jas. Drum. | C | Catholic | 1280 | 830 | 0.648 |
| Dublin, Archbishop | N | Protestant | 2189.5 | 798.5 | 0.364 |
| Agar, John | C | Protestant | 800 | 600 | 0.75 |
| Barry, Sr Jas. | B, C | Protestant | 1160 | 557 | 0.48 |
| Plunkett, Jas. | N, C | Catholic | 1003 | 486 | 0.484 |
| Dublin, City of | C | Protestant | 786 | 470 | 0.597 |
| Barnewall, Jas. | N, C | Protestant | 900 | 448 | 0.497 |
| Hollywood, Nich. | N, B, C | Catholic | 1547 | 427 | 0.27 |
| Fagan, Chris. | B, C | Catholic | 766 | 376 | 0.49 |
| Christchurch | N, B, C | Protestant | 618 | 365 | 0.59 |
| Talbot, John Mal | N, C | Catholic | 501.5 | 300.75 | 0.599 |
| King, Geo. | C | Catholic | 560 | 280 | 0.5 |
| Bolton, Sr Edwd. | N, B, C | Protestant | 700 | 279.5 | 0.399 |
| Netterfield, Luke | N, B | Catholic | 1117 | 275.75 | 0.246 |
| Preston, Robt. | B | Catholic | 1060 | 253 | 0.238 |
| Thomond, Lord | B | Protestant | 1040 | 240 | 0.23 |
| Finglas, John Wpltn | B | Catholic | 731 | 225 | 0.307 |
| Blakeney, Geo. | N, B, C | Catholic | 698 | 217.75 | 0.311 |
| Talbot, Eliz. | B | Catholic | 914 | 207.75 | 0.227 |
| Travers, Wm. | N, B | Catholic | 855 | 183 | 0.214 |
| Bysse, John | N, B, C | Protestant | 692 | 168 | 0.242 |
| Barnewall, Matt. | B | Catholic | 587 | 152.15 | 0.259 |
| Cruse, Chr. | B | Catholic | 672 | 146.4 | 0.217 |
| Gormanstown, Ld | N, B | Catholic | 681 | 146 | 0.214 |
| Finglas, Eliz. | B | Catholic | 617 | 140 | 0.226 |
| Dungan, Edwd. | B | Catholic | 510 | 140 | 0.274 |
| Ormond, Lord | B | Protestant | 760 | 132 | 0.173 |

APPENDIX 3

*Leading Fingallian proprietors ranked by annual rental value per acre*

| Proprietor | Barony | Religion | Acreage | Valuation | £ per acre |
|---|---|---|---|---|---|
| Agar, John | C | Protestant | 800 | 600 | 0.75 |
| Bath, Jas. Drum | C | Catholic | 1280 | 830 | 0.648 |
| Talbot, John Mal | N, C | Catholic | 501.5 | 300.75 | 0.599 |
| Dublin, City of | C | Protestant | 786 | 470 | 0.597 |
| Christchurch | N, B, C | Protestant | 618 | 365 | 0.59 |
| King, Geo. | C | Catholic | 560 | 280 | 0.5 |
| Barnewall, Jas. | N, C | Protestant | 900 | 448 | 0.497 |
| Fagan, Chris. | B, C | Catholic | 766 | 376 | 0.49 |
| Plunkett, Jas. | N, C | Catholic | 1003 | 486 | 0.484 |
| Barry, Sr Jas. | B, C | Protestant | 1160 | 557 | 0.48 |
| Bolton, Sr Edwd. | N, B, C | Protestant | 700 | 279.5 | 0.399 |
| Dublin, Archbishop | N | Protestant | 2189.5 | 798.5 | 0.364 |
| Howth, Thos. Lord | N, B, C | Protestant | 3609 | 1217.5 | 0.337 |
| Barnewall, Nich. | N, B, C | Catholic | 4017.5 | 1308.5 | 0.325 |
| Blakeney, Geo. | N, B, C | Catholic | 698 | 217.75 | 0.311 |
| Finglas, John Wpltn | B | Catholic | 731 | 225 | 0.307 |
| Hollywood, Nich. | N, B, C | Catholic | 1547 | 427 | 0.276 |
| Dungan, Edwd. | B | Catholic | 510 | 140 | 0.274 |
| Barnewall, Matt. | B | Catholic | 587 | 152.15 | 0.259 |
| Netterfield, Luke | N, B | Catholic | 1117 | 275.75 | 0.246 |
| Bysse, John | N, B, C | Protestant | 692 | 168 | 0.242 |
| Preston, Robt. | B | Catholic | 1060 | 253 | 0.238 |
| Thomond, Lord | B | Protestant | 1040 | 240 | 0.23 |
| Talbot, Eliz. | B | Catholic | 914 | 207.75 | 0.227 |
| Finglas, Eliz. | B | Catholic | 617 | 140 | 0.226 |
| Cruse, Chr. | B | Catholic | 672 | 146.4 | 0.217 |
| Gorrnanstown, Ld | N, B | Catholic | 681 | 146 | 0.214 |
| Travers, Wm. | N, B | Catholic | 855 | 183 | 0.214 |
| Ormond, Lord | B | Protestant | 760 | 132 | 0.173 |

# Notes

ABBREVIATIONS

| | |
|---|---|
| Bodl. | Bodleian Library, Oxford |
| B.L. | British Library |
| *Cal. S.P. Ire.* | *Calendar of State Papers, Ireland* |
| Cal. Talbot Mss | Calendar of Talbot manuscripts, Library, Trinity College, Dublin |
| D.K.R. | 'Abstract of decrees of the court of claims for the trial of innocents', in *Nineteenth Report of the Deputy-keeper of public records in Ireland*, (1887), appendix v. |
| H.M.C. | Historical Manuscripts Commission |
| I.R.C.R. | Report of the Irish Record Commission |
| I.M.C. | Irish Manuscripts Commission |
| N.A. | National Archives |
| N.L.I. | National Library of Ireland |
| P.R.O. | Public Record Office, London |
| Submissions and Evidence | J.G. Simms, (ed.), A transcript of the Armagh Public Library Ms, 'Claims of innocence: submissions and evidence, 28 January–20 August 1663', on deposit in the manuscript reading room, Trinity College, Dublin. |

## INTRODUCTION

1 J.G. Simms, 'Land owned by catholics in 1688', in *Irish Historical Studies*, vii, (1951), pp 180–190.

2 Raymond Gillespie, 'A question of survival: the O'Farrells and Longford in the seventeenth century', in Raymond Gillespie and Gerard Moran, (eds), *Longford: Essays in County History*, (Dublin, 1991), p. 13.

3 Bodl., Talbot Ms b.1, f.111.

4 Robert Dunlop, *Ireland under the Commonwealth: being a selection of documents relating to the government of Ireland from 1651 to 1659*, (2 vols, Manchester, 1913).

5 L.J. Arnold, *The Restoration land settlement in county Dublin, 1660–1688*, (Dublin, 1993); Harold O'Sullivan, 'Land ownership changes in the county of Louth in the seventeenth century', unpublished Ph. D. thesis, Trinity College, Dublin, (1993).

## THE TALBOTS OF MALAHIDE AND THEIR WORLD

1 N.A., Books of Survey and Distribution (Quit Rent set), vol. viii (county Dublin), f.92, ff 59–72, vol. vii, (county Louth), ff 229–30.

2 Robert Simington, (ed.), *The Civil Survey 1654–56*, (10 vols., Dublin, 1931–61), vii, p. 16; L.J. Arnold, *The Restoration land settlement*, p. 114.

3 Dublin Corporation Gilbert Library, Gilbert Collection, 14c (23), p. 752.

4   Cal. Talbot Mss, no. 124, p. 188.

5   Simington, *The Civil Survey*, vii, p. 195.

6   Simington, *The Civil Survey*, vii, p. 195.

7   Cal. Talbot Mss, no. 188, p. 189.

8   Simington, *The Civil Survey*, vii, p. 195.

9   Bodl., Talbot Ms c.54, pp 10–12, James Talbot to his son James, 21 October 1846.

10  Bodl., Talbot Ms c.54 p. 2, Charlotte FitzGerald to James Talbot, 18 February 1861.

11  Ella MacMahon, *Historic houses of the United Kingdom*, (London, 1894), p. 92.

12  *Calendar of the Carew Manuscripts preserved in the archiepiscopal library at Lambeth*, (6 vols., London, 1867–73), v (Miscellaneous papers), p. 194.

13  Bodl., Carte Ms 2, p. 469.

14  'Hearth money roll for county Dublin', in *Kildare Archaeological Journal*, xi, (1929–33), p. 386 *et seq.*

15  Bodl., Talbot Ms c.54, pp 10–12, James Talbot to his son James, 21 October 1846.

16  Bodl., Talbot Ms c.54, p. 2, Charlotte FitzGerald to her nephew James, 18 February, 1861: 'My great-grand-mother (Francis, daughter of Sir Robert Talbot of Carton), wishing to modernise the castle built up straight some battlements and new-fashioned some of the windows'.

17  George Little, 'About Malahide', in *Dublin Historical Record*, x, no. 1, pt. 1, (March-May, 1948), p. 5 ; John D'Alton, *The history of the county of Dublin*, (Dublin, 1838), p. 95.

18  Submissions and Evidence, no. 918.

19  John Dunton, *Teague Land , or A Merry Ramble to the Wild Irish: Letters from Ireland, 1698*, edited by Edward MacLysaght, (Dublin, 1982), pp 54–5.

20  Simington, *The Civil Survey*, vii, p. 195.

21  Seamus Pender (ed.), *A census of Ireland, circa 1659*, (Dublin, 1939), is now generally accepted to be a statistical abstract of the 1660 poll tax returns. For a review of the evidence relating to this question, see S.T. Carleton, *Heads and hearths: the hearth money rolls and poll tax returns for county Antrim 1660–69*, (Belfast 1991), pp xi–xii.

22  Carleton, *Heads and hearths*, pp xi–xii, 175.

23  H.MC, *Egmont Mss*, i, pt.1, p. 171; Cal. Talbot Mss, no. 278, p. 225.

24  Cal. Talbot Mss, no.219, p. 269.

25  Simington, *The Civil Survey*, vii, p. 195.

26  'Hearth money roll for county Dublin', pp 388–9.

27  Carleton, *Heads and hearths*, p. xii.

28  Pender, *A census of Ireland circa 1659*, p. 388.

29  L.M. Cullen, 'Population trends in seventeenth century Ireland', in *Economic and Social Review*, vi, 2, (1975), p. 153 n.

30  Carleton, *Heads and hearths*, p. xi.

31  Cal. Talbot Mss, no. 278, p. 225.

32  Pender, *A census of Ireland circa 1659*, p. 388. For Cotton's commission under the Poll Ordinance of April 1660, see p. 621.

33  B.L., Egerton Ms 1762, f. 116; Rowley Lascelles, *Liber munerum publicorum Hiberniae*, (2 vols., London, 1810), i, pt.2, p. 147; Cal. Talbot Mss, no. 372.

34  Lascelles, *Liber munerum publicorum Hiberniae*, i, pt.2, p. 147.

35  Dunton, *Teague Land*, p. 55.

36  Cal. Talbot Mss, no.219, p. 269; Pender, *A census of Ireland circa 1659*, p. 388; H.M.C., *Egmont Mss*, i, pt. 1, p. 171; 'Hearth money roll for county Dublin', pp 388–9; Dunton, *Teague Land*, p. 56.

37  'Hearth money roll for county Dublin', pp 388–9.

38  Dunton, *Teague Land*, p. 55.

39  Dunton, *Teague Land*, p. 58.

40  Bodl., Carte Ms 2, f. 469, Ormond to the lords justices, 15 March, 1642;

The Down Survey reference is quoted from Weston St. John Joyce, *The neighbourhood of Dublin*, (Dublin, 1939), p. 280.

41  Dunton, *Teague Land*, p. 56.

42  H.F. Berry, (ed.), *Register of wills and inventories of the diocese of Dublin 1457–1483*, (R.S.A.I., extra volume, Dublin, 1896–7), p. 83–4.

43  H.M.C., *A catalogue of the Shrewsbury and Talbot papers*, (2 vols., London, 1971), ii, p. 185.

44  John Dunton, *The Dublin Scuffle*, (London, 1699), p. 371.

45  Dunton, *Teague Land*, p. 55.

46  Dunton, *Teague Land*, pp. 54–5.

47  Dunton, *Teague Land*, p. 56.

48  Bodl., Talbot Ms a.1; Cal. Talbot Mss, no. 426, p. 617. March 1786, Col. Richard Talbot lets eleven acres to William Clinch of Malahide with the condition that the tenant 'shall do suit and service and attend the manor courts and pay the usual fine or homage money'.

49  Bodl., Talbot Ms a.1.

50  Cal. Talbot Mss, no. 219, p. 268.

51  Mary Ellis, *Using manorial records*, (London, 1994), p. 53.

52  Bodl., Talbot Ms c.54, pp 10–12. James Talbot to his son James, 21 October 1846.

53  Cal. Talbot Mss, no. 182, p. 172.

54  Cal. Talbot Mss, no. 219, p. 268; Submissions and Evidence, no. 175.

55  Cal. Talbot Mss, no. 192, p. 202.

56  Cal. Talbot Mss, no. 309, p. 422.

57  Cal. Talbot Mss, no. 309, p. 429.

58  Cal. Talbot Mss, no. 404, p. 582. Indenture between Richard Talbot and Francis Smith of Balregan, 1774. 'Francis Smith undertakes to grind his corn, grain, grist or malt. at the mill of Malahide ... and to pay the usual toll or mulcture'.

59  Simington, *The Civil Survey*, vii. Fingal comprised by estimation a total of 48,489 acres of which 33,271 acres were assigned to arable farm-ing, 8,727 acres to pasture and 2,112 acres to meadow. The remainder consisted of woodland, furze, conny-warrens and unprofitable land.

60  Simington, *The Civil Survey*, vii, p. 195.

61  Margaret C. Griffith, (ed.), *Calendar of inquisitions formerly in the office of the chief remembrancer of the exchequer prepared from the mss of the Irish record commission*, (Dublin, 1991), p. 52.

62  N.A., Books of survey and distribu-tion, (Quit Rent set), vol. viii, f.66; Cal. Talbot Mss, no. 309, p. 430.

63  Cal. Talbot Mss, no. 309, p. 429.

64  Berry, *Register of wills*, p. 83–4.

65  John De Courcy Ireland, *Ireland's sea fisheries: a history*, (Dublin, 1981), p. 16.

66  De Courcy Ireland, *Ireland's sea fish-eries*, p. 16, p. 18.

67  Berry, *Register of wills*, p. 83–4.

68  Bodl., Talbot Ms c.54, p. 60.

69  R.R. Steele, *Tudor and Stuart Proclamations*, (2 vols., Oxford, 1910), ii, pt.1, no. 370, p. 44; B.L., Egerton Ms 1761, f. 1; NLI, mf p. 576.

70  Bodl., Carte Ms 2, f. 469.

71  Bodl., Carte Ms 2, f. 474.

72  Bodl., Talbot Ms a.1.

73  Bodl., Talbot Ms c.54, p. 60.

74  Bodl., Talbot Ms a.1.

75  Bodl., Talbot Ms c.95, no. 6.

76  Bodl., Talbot Ms b.49, no. 10.

77  Dalton, *The history of the county of Dublin*, p. 98; M.V. Ronan, 'Archbishop Bulkeley's visitation of Dublin, 1630', in *Archivium Hibernicum*, viii, (1941), pp 67–8.

78  Cal. Talbot Mss, no. 348, p. 492, refers to a 1733 lease of the oys-terbed at the rent of £12 yearly; Cal. Talbot Mss, no. 613, p. 901, Indenture, 1 May 1835, Richard Talbot lets to Henry Murphy *et al*, the oyster bed for a yearly rent of £110 and 5,000 marketable oysters to be delivered to lessor every year.

79  Cal. Talbot Mss, no. 348, p. 492; Bodl., Talbot Ms c.54, p. 2.

80 Bodl., Carte Ms 2, f. 469

81 P. R.O., SP 63/304/311.

82 P. R.O., SP 63/304/311.

83 Cal. Talbot Mss, no. 188, p. 186.

84 Cal. Talbot Mss, no. 188, p. 184.

85 Cal. Talbot Mss, no. 188. The replication of the plaintiff, Sir John Talbot, to the answer of Richard Talbot.

86 G.D. Burtchaell, and T.U. Sadleir, (eds.), *Alumni Dublinenses*, (London, 1924), p. 799; Donal F. Cregan, 'Irish Catholic admissions to the English Inns of Court, 1558–1625' in *Irish Jurist*, v, n.s., (1970), pp 95–113.

87 N.A., Miscellaneous deeds, Box 2/499/28, no. 1, deed of feeoffment, 1 February, 1619.

88 Cal. Talbot Mss, no. 218, p. 265, last will of Richard Talbot, 26 July 1640.

89 Nicholas P. Canny, *The formation of the Old English elite in Ireland*, (Dublin, 1975), p. 33.

90 Colm Lennon, *Richard Stanihurst the Dubliner, 1547–1618*, (Dublin, 1981), p. 145.

91 *Cal. S.P. Ire, 1509–1573*, p. 71.

92 Genealogical Office, Dublin, Mss 47, 48, 79; Tom O'Shea, *The Talbots and Malahide Castle*, (Dublin, 1992), pp 136–7; Dublin Corporation Gilbert Library, Gilbert collection, *Genealogical memoir of the antient and noble family of Talbot of Malahide in the county of Dublin*, (Dublin, 1829).

93 Bodl., Talbot Ms c.54, p. 2.

94 For a blatant example see *Cal. S.P. Ire., 1663–65*, p. 674, Col Dick Talbot to Joseph Williamson; 'As soon as the business is done ... I shall get you 100 pieces by it in land or money to begin your Irish estate with. I hope we shall in time make a good one of it'; L.J. Arnold, *The Restoration land settlement in county Dublin*, pp 72–3.

95 *Cal. Carew Mss*, v, p. 194; *The Irish fiants of the Tudor sovereigns during the reigns of Henry VIII, Edward VI, Philip & Mary and Elizabeth I*, (3 vols., Dublin, 1994), nos. 542, 2117, 3182, 4148.

96 N.A., RC, 10/3, vii, p. 41.

97 Cal. Talbot Mss, no. 88, p. 185.

98 Cal. Talbot Mss, no. 182, p. 172.

99 J.T. Gilbert and Lady Gilbert, (eds.), *Calendar of the ancient records of Dublin in the possession of the municipal corporation*, (19 vols., Dublin, 1889–1944), i, p. 176.

100 Cal. Talbot Mss, no. 216, p. 251.

101 Arnold, *The Restoration land settlement*, p. 24; *Cal. Carew Mss*, v, p. 194.

102 Ronan, 'Archbishop Bulkeley's visitation of Dublin, 1630', pp 67–8.

103 R.C. Simington and John McLellan, 'Oireachtas Library, list of outlaws, 1641–1647', in *Analecta Hibernica*, 23, (1966), p. 344.

104 Berry, *Register of wills*, p. 83–4.

105 William E. Vandeleur, *Notes on Malahide*, (Dublin, 1915), p. 6.

106 George Little, 'About Malahide', in *Dublin Historical Record*, x, no. 1, pt. 1, (March-May, 1948), p. 5; D'Alton, *The history of the county Dublin*, p. 95.

107 Bodl., Talbot Ms b.1, f.111.

108 J.F. Shearman, 'Patrician missionaries in Leinster', in *The Journal of the Royal Historical and Archeological Association of Ireland*, iii, 4th series, (1874–5), p. 405 n; Bodl., Talbot Ms b.1, f.111, Ms c.54, p. 18.

109 J.T. Gilbert, (ed.), *Chartularies of St. Mary's Abbey, Dublin*, (2 vols., London 1857), i, pp 129–30.

110 Tom O'Shea, *The Talbots and Malahide Castle*, (Dublin, 1992), pp 36–7.

111 Bodl., Talbot Ms b.1, f.111. John Talbot believed the statue to be in the house at the time of his pilgrimage to Portmarnock. In the rhapsody he is reported as being sorry that he could not visit the image 'by Corbet's lieving in ye house'. For a far-fetched theory

which claimed that the statue was invisible because of smoke from the chimney, see Bodl., Talbot Ms c.54, p. 2.

### WAR AND TRANSPLANTATION
### 1641–1659

1  M. Perceval-Maxwell, *The outbreak of the Irish Rebellion of 1641*, (Dublin, 1994), p. 253; H.M.C., *Ormonde Mss*, n.s. 2, (1903), p. 22, Lords Justices and Council to the earl of Leicester (Lord Lieutenant), 25 November 1641.

2  John Temple, *The Irish rebellion*, (London, 1646), pp 139–41.

3  H.M.C., *Ormonde Mss*, n.s. ii, p. 31, Lords Justices and Council to the earl of Leicester, 30 November 1641; J.T. Gilbert, *History of the Irish Confederation and the war in Ireland, 1641–1643*, (7 vols., Dublin, 1882–91), iii, p. 334–6, Sir Patrick Wemys to Ormonde, 1 December 1641.

4  Temple, *The Irish rebellion*, p. 147; H.M.C., *Ormonde Mss*, n.s.ii, p. 36, Lords Justices and Council to earl of Leicester, 14 December 1641.

5  *Cal S.p. Ire, 1663–65*, pp 172–3.

6  Temple, *The Irish rebellion*, p. 143.

7  Temple, *The Irish rebellion*, p. 149; Patrick Archer, *Fair Fingall*, (Dublin, n.d.), p. 71.

8  Temple, *The Irish rebellion*, p. 151, Lords Justices to Luke Netterville, Blackney, George King *et al*, 9 December 1641; H.M.C., *Ormonde Mss*, n.s. ii, p. 38, Lords Justices and Council to the earl of Leicester, 14 December 1641.

9  Trinity College, Dublin Mss, 809, 810.

10  Gilbert, *History of the Irish confederation*, iii, p. 382.

11  H.M.C, *Ormonde Mss*, n.s. ii, p. 38, Lords Justices and Council to the earl of Leicester, 14 December 1641.

12  Gilbert, *History of the Irish Confederation*, i, p. 229–30, Gentry of the English Pale to Lord Justices and Council of Ireland, 10 December 1641.

13  Steele, *Tudor and Stuart Proclamations*, no. 357, p. 42.

14  Trinity College, Dublin, Ms 810, f.214, deposition by David Powell taken on 14 December 1641; Steele, *Tudor and Stuart Proclamations*, ii, pt.1, no. 358a. This proclamation, authorising the attack on Clontarf, is dated 14 Dec 1641.

15  H.M.C., *Ormonde Mss*, n.s.ii, p. 48, Lords Justices and Council to the earl of Leicester, 28 December 1641; H.M.C., *Egmont Mss*, i, pt.1, p. 158, Sir Paul Davys to Sir Philip Percivall, 1 January 1642.

16  H.M.C., *Ormonde Mss*, n.s. ii, p. 39, Lords Justices and Council to the earl of Leicester, 14 December 1641.

17  H.M.C., *Ormonde Mss*, n.s. ii, p. 45, Lords Justices and Council to the earl of Leicester, 28 December 1641; H.M.C., *Egmont Mss*, i, pt.1, pp 159–60, Sir Paul Davys to Sir Philip Percivall, 11 January 1642.

18  Gilbert, *History of the Irish Confederation*, i, pp 245–7, Petitions from Lord Dunsany and other prisoners at Dublin.

19  Steele, *Tudor and Stuart Proclamations*, ii, pt. 1, no. 358, p. 42 ; Gilbert, *History of the Irish Confederation*, i, pp 229–30.

20  Gilbert, *History of the Irish Confederation*, i, pp 245–7.

21  Trinity College, Dublin, Ms 810, f.382, f.386, f.391.

22  Gilbert, *History of the Irish Confederation*, iii, p. 382.

23  Submissions and Evidence, no. 88.

24  Perceval-Maxwell, *The outbreak of the Irish Rebellion of 1641*, p. 223.

25  Submissions and Evidence, no. 88.

26  Submissions and Evidence, no. 175.

27 Thomas Carte, *The life of James duke of Ormond*, (new edition, 6 vols., Oxford, 1851), ii, p. 467.

28 Steele, *Tudor and Stuart Proclamations*, ii, pt. 1, no. 360, p. 42.

29 *The particular relation of the present estate and condition of Ireland as now it stands manifested by severall letters sent for and to such persons as may give full satisfaction of the truth*, Adam Loftus to Sir Robert King, 14 February 1642.

30 Gilbert, *History of the Irish Confederation*, iii, p. 382.

31 Its formal title was 'An act for the speedy and effectual reducing of the rebels in His Majesty's Kingdom of Ireland', *Statutes of the Realm*, (London, 1810–28), 16 Car. I, c.33.

32 H.M.C., *Ormonde Mss*, o.s.i, (1899), pp 136–143.

33 Bodl., Carte Ms 2, ff. 469, 474.

34 Bodl., Carte Ms 2, ff. 469, 474; H.M.C., *Ormonde Mss*, o.s.i, p. 136, p. 138, p. 143.

35 P. R.O., SP 63/304/312.

36 *Fynes Moryson's itinerary*, (new edition, Glasgow, 1908), iv, pp 188–9.

37 Steele, *Tudor and Stuart Proclamations*, ii, pt. 1, no. 370, p. 44.

38 Gilbert, *History of the Irish Confederation*, ii, p. 209.

39 Steele, *Tudor and Stuart Proclamations*, ii, pt. 1, p. 45, nos. 375, 377, 379.

40 Gilbert, *History of the Irish confederation*, ii, p. 209.

41 For this practice see Steele, *Tudor and Stuart Proclamations*, ii, pt.i, no. 375, p. 45, a proclamation dated 31 December 1642 which refers to persons 'holding rebels' towns and lands by way of custodium from the king'.

42 *Cal. S. P. Ireland, 1633–47*, pp 378, 385, 388.

43 P. R.O., SP 63/304/311.

44 J.T. Gilbert, *A contemporary history of the affairs in Ireland, from A.D. 1641–52*, ( 3 vols., Dublin, 1879), iii, pp 300–303.

45 P. R.O., SP 63/304/311.

46 P. R.O., SP 63/304/311.

47 Edward McLysaght, 'Commonwealth State Accounts', in *Analecta Hibernica*, 15, (1944), p. 245.

48 P. R.O., SP 63/304/311.

49 B.L., Egerton Ms 1761, f. 1.

50 Steele, *Tudor and Stuart Proclamations*, i, pt.i, nos. 515, 500, 503, 515, pp 62–4.

51 Steele, *Tudor and Stuart Proclamations*, ii, pt.i, no. 515, p. 64; Dunlop, *Commonwealth*, doc.380, p. 340.

52 Dunlop, *Commonwealth*, doc.351, p. 324.

53 McLysaght, 'Commonwealth State Accounts', p. 245.

54 Cal. Talbot Mss, no. 309, p. 248.

55 Cal. Talbot Mss, no. 225, p. 278.

56 Cal. Talbot Mss, no. 225, p. 278.

57 H.M.C., *Ormonde Mss*, n.s. ii, pp 400–405.

58 McLysaght, 'Commonwealth State Accounts', p. 245.

59 B.L., Egerton Ms.1762, f. 30.

60 Cal. Talbot Mss, no. 284, p. 230.

61 Henry Scobell, *A collection of acts and ordinances of general use made in the parliament begun and held at Westminster, the third day of November 1640 and since, unto the adjournment of the parliament begun and holden the 17th of September, anno 1650*, (London, 1658), cap. 13, pp. 197–200.

62 S.R. Gardiner, 'The Transplantation to Connacht' in *English Historical Review*, xiv (1899), pp 702–4; P.J. Corish, 'The Cromwellian Regime 1650–60', in T.W. Moody, F.X. Martin and F.J. Byrne, (eds), *A new history of Ireland*, iii, *Early modern Ireland 1534–1691*, (Oxford 1976), p. 359.

63 Scobell, *Acts and Ordinances*, cap. 13, p. 199.

64 Dunlop, *Commonwealth*, doc. 400, pp 355–9; C.H. Firth and R.S. Rait, (eds.), *Acts and ordinances of the Interregnum, 1642–1660*, (2 vols, London, 1911), ii, p. 722 ff.

65  Dunlop, *Commonwealth*, doc.502, p. 482; R.C. Simington, *The transplantation to Connacht, 1654–58*, (Dublin, 1970), p. xi.

66  Dunlop, *Commonwealth*, doc.446, pp 387–8.

67  Dunlop, *Commonwealth*, doc.446, pp 387–8.

68  Dunlop, *Commonwealth*, doc.587, p. 469.

69  Simington, *Transplantation*, p. xxi; Dunlop, *Commonwealth*, doc.686, pp 522–3.

70  P.J. Corish, 'The Cromwellian Regime 1650–60', in Moody, Martin, Byrne, *A new history of Ireland*, iii, p. 368; See also Simington, *Transplantation*, p. xxiii, for a list of proprietors named in the Act of 1652 as being exempted for pardon for life and estate who nevertheless received large estates in Connacht.

71  Dunlop, *Commonwealth*, doc.576, p. 466, (21 December, 1654). This proclamation was bracketed by a series of threatening directives, see Steele, *Tudor and Stuart Proclamations*, no. 540, p. 66, (30 November, 1654) which warned of arrest and court martial and no. 548, p. 67, (7 March, 1655) threatening the forfeiture of all crops for failure to transplant.

72  Cal. Talbot Mss, no. 226, p. 279.

73  Cal. Talbot Mss, no. 226, p. 279.

74  B.L., Egerton Ms 1762, f. 155.

75  P. R.O., SP 63/304/311.

76  Cal. Talbot Mss, no.227, p. 280.

77  Dunlop, *Commonwealth*, doc.1050, p. 712.

78  Bodl., Talbot Ms b.1, f.111.

79  Bodl., Talbot Ms b.1, f.111.

80  P. R.O., SP 63/304/311.

81  Scobell, *Acts and Ordinances*, p. 198; Simington, *Transplantation*, p. xxiii.

82  H.M.C., *Ormonde Mss*, o.s.ii, p. 161, An Accompt of Lands set out to the Transplanted Irish in Connaught.

83  Simington, *Transplantation*, p. 234, p. 245, p. 270.

84  Dunlop, *Commonwealth*, doc. 846, pp 609–11.

85  N.A., Books of survey and distribution, vol. xx, ff 297–8.

86  Simington, *Transplantation*, p. 275.

87  Pender, *A census of Ireland, circa 1659*, p. 589.

88  N.A., Books of survey and distribution, vol. xx, ff 297–8; I.R.C.R., 15th Report, *Index of persons in the grants under the Acts of Settlement and Explanation*, (1825), p. 244.

89  Bodl., Talbot Ms c.92, f.19; Cal Talbot Mss, no.353; See also Cal. Talbot Mss, no. 309, p. 421, the testimony of Thomas Warren: 'Captain Barton treated with Richard Talbot, deceased, about the purchase of the manor of Castlering and after some time fell off, telling deponent it was not worth sixpence to any man to purchase said estate'.

90  Peter Berresford Ellis, *Hell or Connaught! The Cromwellian colonisation of Ireland 1652–1660*, (London, 1975), pp 234–5.

91  Dunlop, *Commonwealth*, doc.791, pp 569–70, records the commission of an inquiry into the activities of James Shaen and Stephen Squibb, former commissioners at Loughrea, who had taken out custodiums on land in Connacht and let them at inflated rents to transplanters desperate to secure a holding.

SURVIVING THE PEACE 1660–1671

1  J.G. Simms, 'The restoration, 1660–85', in Moody, Martin, Byrne, *A new history of Ireland*, iii, pp 421–2.

2  Karl S. Bottigheimer, 'The restoration land settlement: a structural view' in *Irish Historical Studies*, xviii, (1972–3), p. 9.

3  Bottigheimer, 'The restoration land settlement: a structural view', p. 3; W.D. Macray, *(ed.), Notes which*

passed at meetings of the privy council between Charles II and the earl of Clarendon, *1660–7*, (London, 1896), p. 498.

4   Pender, *A census of Ireland circa 1659*, p. 387; Steele, *Tudor and Stuart Proclamations*, ii, pt. i, no. 573, p. 70, no. 596, p. 73.

5   W.H. Hardinge, 'Observations on the earliest known manuscript census returns of the people of Ireland', in *Royal Irish Academy, Transactions.*, xxiv, (1864), p. 322. The Talbots were certainly resident in 1661 for in attempting to prove the authenticity of the 'census' of 1659 Hardinge notes the name of John Talbot against Malahide on a subsidy roll for county Dublin for that year; For Corbett's Commonwealth rent see Cal. Talbot Mss, 284, p. 230.

6   Arnold, *The Restoration land settlement*, p. 114; Cal. Talbot Mss, no. 230, p. 284.

7   Simms, 'The restoration, 1660–85', in Moody, Martin, Byrne, *A new history of Ireland*, iii, p. 425.

8   Arnold, *The Restoration land settlement*, p. 114.

9   Dublin Corporation Gilbert Library, Gilbert Collection, Ms 198, 2/6, F, p. 237. Dr. John Bastwick, physician and puritan fanatic, lost his ears in the pillory at Westminster in 1637 as a consequence of his scurrilous denunciations of the (Anglican) hierarchy, whom he described, amongst other choice expressions, as 'the fishmongers of the elect of Christ', H. Trevor-Roper, *Archbishop Laud, 1573–1645*, (2nd edition, New York, 1965), pp 317–20.

10  *Irish statutes revised edition, 3rd Edward II to the Union*, (London, 1885), 17 & 18 Charles II. c.2, Clause CXLIII, p. 251.

11  J.P. Prendergast, 'Some account of Sir Audley Mervyn, his Majesty's prime sergeant and speaker in the house of commons in Ireland from 1661 till 1666', in *Royal Historical Society, Transactions*, iii, new series, (1874), p. 423.

12  Harold O'Sullivan, 'The restoration land settlement in the diocese of Armagh , 1660 to 1684' in *Seanchas Ard Mhacha*, xvi, no. 1, (1994), p. 12.

13  H.M.C., *8th Report*, Appendix, (1881), p. 508.

14  O' Sullivan, 'Land ownership changes in the county of Louth', p. 295.

15  O' Sullivan, 'The restoration land settlement in the diocese of Armagh, 1660 to 1684', p. 53.

16  Bodl., Carte Ms 37, p. 64.

17  I.R.C.R., xv, p. 194; Submissions and Evidence, no.175; D.K.R. no. 164.

18  Cal. Talbot Mss, no.229, pp 282–3.

19  Arnold, *The Restoration land settlement*, p. 41; *The Irish Statutes: revised edition*, 14 & 15 Charles II c.2, pp 90–106.

20  Arnold, *The Restoration land settlement*, p. 42.

21  Bodl., Carte Ms 31, f. 95.

22  Bodl., Talbot Ms b.1, no. 9.

23  Bodl., Talbot Ms b.1, no. 9.

24  *Cal. S.P. Ire., 1660–1662*, pp 106, 198.

25  *Cal. S.P. Ire., 1660–1662*, pp 235–6.

26  *Cal. S.P. Ire., 1660–1662*, pp 356, 561

27  *Cal. S.P. Ire., 1660–1662*, p. 660.

28  *The Irish Statutes: revised edition*, 14 & 15 Charles II c.2, p. 99, p. 102, p. 175.

29  *The Irish Statutes: revised edition*, 14 & 15 Charles II c.2, p. 117, p. 164.

30  Cal. Talbot Mss, no. 284, p. 230.

31  N.A., D.11412.

32  Bodl., Talbot Ms c.92, no. 19.

33  *Journal of the house of commons of the kingdom of Ireland*, (Dublin, 1796), i, p. 612.

34  D'Alton, *The history of the county of Dublin*, p. 99; Bodl., Talbot Ms b.48, no. 10.

35  W.H. Hardinge, 'Observations on the earliest known manuscript census returns of the people of Ireland',

p. 322; H.M.C., *8th Report,*
Appendix, (1881), p. 508; 'Hearth
money roll for county Dublin',
p. 388.

36  Lascelles, *Liber munerum publicorum
Hiberniae,* i, pt.2, p. 147.

37  Cal. Talbot Mss, no.286, p. 232; For
evidence of other Borr loans see
O'Sullivan, 'The restoration land
settlement in the diocese of
Armagh, 1660 to 1684'.

38  Submissions and Evidence, no. 175,
p. 104–5; I.R.C.R., viii, supp., p. 293.

39  Submissions and Evidence, no.175;
O'Sullivan, 'Land ownership changes
in the county of Louth', p. 294.

40  Cal. Talbot Mss, no. 218, p. 265.

41  Submissions and Evidence, no. 175.

42  Submissions and Evidence, no. 918.

43  *Journal of the house of commons of the
kingdom of Ireland,* i, pp 614–31.

44  Richard Talbot of Carton was the
great-grandson of Sir Peter Talbot of
Malahide. His father William was
closely associated with John Talbot's
father, also Richard, both of whom
acted as legal advisers to the earl of
Kildare. Nicholas Plunkett was the
brother of Luke Plunkett, 1st earl of
Fingall.

45  Dublin Corporation Gilbert
Library, Gilbert Collection, Ms 198,
2/6, F, p. 200.

46  Dublin Corporation Gilbert
Library, Gilbert Collection, Ms 198,
2/6, F p. 237.

47  *Irish statutes: revised edition,* 17 & 18
Charles II. c.2, Clause CXLIII, p. 251.

48  Cal. Talbot Mss, no. 241, p. 300.

49  Arnold, *The Restoration land settlement,* p. 106.

50  *Inquisitionum in officio rotulorum can-
cellariae Hiberniae asservatorum repertorium,* i, 16 Jac II, no. 16 (Dublin).

51  Cal Talbot Mss, no. 309, p. 421.

52  Bodl. Talbot Ms c.91, no. 9;
Submissions and Evidence, no. 175.

53  N.A., D.11412.

54  O'Sullivan, 'Land ownership changes
in the county of Louth', p. 295.

55  Bodl., Talbot Ms c.92, f.19; Cal
Talbot Mss, no. 353.

56  *Cal. S.P. Ire., 1666–69,* p. 683; Bodl.,
Talbot Ms e.10, no. 305, p. 70.

57  Cal. Talbot Mss, no. 309, p. 424.

58  For an example of this see, John
Kingston, 'Catholic families of the
Pale' in *Repertorium Novum,* ii, no. 1,
(1958), pp 99–101.

59  N.A., Books of survey and distribution, (Quit rent office set), viii, f. 72.

60  Simington, *The Civil Survey,* vii,
p. 14, pp 40–1, pp 75–6.

61  The data contained in the appendices has been extrapolated from the
county Dublin volume of *The Civil
Survey* and comprises the aggregated
acreage and annual rental value of
each proprietor's holdings in the
baronies of Coolock, Nethercross
and Balrothery. These figures are es-
timates and therefore can only be
relied on to provide general, rather
than definitive, conclusions. John
Talbot's Malahide estate in county
Dublin was estimated by the Civil
Survey commissioners to comprise
500 acres. Here it is registered as
501.5 acres, to include a small parcel
of 1.5 acres which the commissioners attributed to him in Swords, in
the barony of Nethercross.